THE MANAGEMENT OF
FAILING DIPSW STUDENTS

The Management of Failing DipSW Students

Activities and exercises to prepare practice teachers for work with failing students

MAVIS SHARP
and
HAZEL DANBURY

Ashgate

ARENA

Aldershot • Brookfield USA • Singapore • Sydney

Published by
Ashgate Publishing Limited
Gower House
Croft Road
Aldershot
Hants GU11 3HR
England

Ashgate Publishing Company
Old Post Road
Brookfield
Vermont 05036
USA

British Library Cataloguing in Publication Data
Sharp, Mavis
    The management of failing DipSW students : activities and
    exercises to prepare practice teachers for work with
    failing students
    1. Social work education – Great Britain
    I. Title II. Danbury, Hazel, 1939–
    361'.00711'41

Library of Congress
Sharp, Mavis, 1945–
    The management of failing DipSW students : activities and
    exercises to prepare teachers for work with failing
    students / Mavis Sharp and Hazel Danbury.
        p.   cm.
    Includes bibliographical references (p.   ).
    ISBN 1-85742-437-9 (pbk.)
    1. Social work education—Great Britain.   2. Student teaching—
    Great Britain.   3. Grading and marking (Students)—Great Britain.
    4. Grading and marking (Students)—Great Britain—Problems,
    exercises, etc.   5. School failure—Great Britain.   I. Danbury,
    Hazel, 1939– .   II. Title.   III. Title: Management of failing
    Diploma in Social Work students.
    HV11.8.G7S53   1999
    361.31'2'071141—dc21   98-51475
                                                                         CIP

ISBN 1 85742 437 9

Typeset in Great Britain by Manton Typesetters, Louth, Lincolnshire.
Printed and bound by Athenaeum Press, Ltd.,
Gateshead, Tyne & Wear.

Contents

Dedication   *vi*
Acknowledgements   *vii*
Lists of activities, boxes, exercises and figures   *viii*

Introduction   1
1   A review of social work training   5
2   Practice teaching and the DipSW assessment process   11
3   Assessment of failure   29
4   The decision to fail   51
5   Good enough practice   79
6   Telling the student and recording the decision   97
7   The support needs of practice teachers   119
8   Problems in placements   143
9   Ready or not?   171

Bibliography   185
Index   189

Dedication

This book commemorates Hazel Danbury. She was a co-author in its early planning stages. Sadly she died in August 1997, after a courageous struggle against a debilitating condition, which gave her a thorough understanding of disability and its effects.

Hazel was a close friend and professional colleague of many years standing. A week before she died, when virtually bereft of all faculties, she still managed to encourage me to get on and finish this book – so I have.

This typified the support and frequent inspiration she gave over many years to both social work students and practice teachers.

Acknowledgements

To Peter Sharp and Rochelle Fisher for their proof reading, Jean Morton and Nigel Horner for their consultation, Hazel's sons Christopher and Richard who ensured I could access their mother's training materials and John Toplin for his patient support when my IT skills proved deficient!

Lists of activities, boxes, exercises and figures

Activities

Activity 2.1	Identifying cause for complaint	18
Activity 3.1	Where are you?	39
Activity 3.2	Identifying knowledge and skills	41
Activity 3.3	Self-development exercise on assessment	42
Activity 3.4	Exchanging ideas on assessment	44
Activity 4.1	Ground rules	57
Activity 4.2	Preparation for direct observation	64
Activity 5.1	Identifying minimal levels of practice	85
Activity 5.2	Thinking around failure	87
Activity 6.1	Stereotypes of students	103
Activity 6.2	Breaking bad news	106
Activity 6.3	Is this report good enough?	112
Activity 7.1	Tutor's visit to a placement	126
Activity 7.2	What do I do?	135
Activity 7.3	Maze of support	136
Activity 8.1	Expectations regarding students on placement	144
Activity 8.2	Problems on placement	162
Activity 8.3	Dealing with problems	163
Activity 9.1	Identifying training needs for work with failing students	173
Activity 9.2	Engaging with failure	175
Activity 9.3	Team readiness to take a failing student	177

Boxes

Box 2.1	A sample Practice Assessment Panel assessment report	27
Box 3.1	Outline for recording a practice teaching session	37

Box 4.1   Sample format for feedback on direct observation of
           practice   63
Box 4.2   Sample pro forma for direct observation of practice by
           colleagues   68
Box 5.1   Checklist: Positive and negative indicators of competence   83
Box 5.2   Guidelines for identifying appropriate levels of student
           competence by the end of each placement, linked to the
           values which CCETSW requires for each practice
           requirement   84
Box 5.3   Checklist: Has the placement been adequate?   93
Box 6.1   Sample practice teacher profile (adapted from Danbury 1994) 101
Box 6.2   Checklist: The principles of giving feedback   109
Box 7.1   Sample model for a black consultancy to a placement –
           guidelines for an agreement   134
Box 8.1   Procedures in the event of a malpractice allegation by a
           student on placement (from the Nottingham Trent
           University DipSW Practice Teacher Handbook, 1998)   170

Exercises

Exercise 2.1   Becoming familiar with procedures   24
Exercise 2.2   Further practice in procedures for failure   26
Exercise 3.1   Making a contract on assessment   48
Exercise 4.1   Direct observation: advantages and disadvantages   72
Exercise 4.2   Preparation for direct observation   73
Exercise 4.3   Further preparation for direct observation   74
Exercise 4.4   Practising assessment in direct observation   76
Exercise 5.1   Assessing good enough practice   93
Exercise 5.2   Is our practice good enough?   95
Exercise 6.1   Role play on giving feedback   115
Exercise 6.2   Practice in giving feedback   116
Exercise 6.3   Report writing   117
Exercise 7.1   Discussion: What do I do?   138
Exercise 7.2   Ground rules when support is needed   141
Exercise 8.1   Dealing with problems in placement   167
Exercise 8.2   More work with placement problems   169
Exercise 9.1   Ready or not?   181

Figures

Figure 2.1   Diagrammatic summary of one process for failing
              students   13
Figure 4.1   Ground rules for direct observation   65

Introduction

The task of failing a social work student can be a stressful, complex, yet a highly necessary part of practice teaching.

The decision to write this book stems from our joint extensive experience in practice teacher training, placement development and university teaching in social work. This leads us to the view that practice teachers frequently find the assessment of a failing or borderline student a daunting experience. They will often avoid accepting such a student on placement, even if they are experienced and competent to do so. Inexperienced and new practice teachers often regard as their nightmare scenario the possibility of working with a student who turns out to be at risk of failure.

Our experience also informs us that practice teacher training does not ignore the issues pertinent to failing students, but it tends to focus on individual student assessment. It often treats failure and its concomitant losses as a discrete area of training, instead of permeating it through the entire process. Similarly situations where the placement as a whole gets into difficulties can be marginalised. Placement briefing workshops for practice teachers and students can avoid any mention of failure, despite it being one potential outcome for all placements. It can instead be treated as a taboo, and disregarded, because of its potential for raising anxieties, although its likelihood can often be a hidden agenda for all participants at the initial placement meeting, and throughout the placement process.

The purpose of this book therefore is to provide a reference manual for practice teachers who are, or potentially could be, involved in the process of failing students. It sets out information on the process, as well as some of the problems and suggestions for handling them. The focus is not just on making the assessment decision regarding an individual student, but also on the management of the whole failing process, and the problems and challenges it can bring.

An initial outline will be given on the background to the current Diploma in Social Work (DipSW) assessment framework, and how it can compound dilemmas for practice teachers in the area of failing students. Consideration is then given to relevant aspects involved in the process of failing students.

We have chosen to handle this topic as a reference manual, because it focuses on the assessment function of practice teaching, which is more prescribed. As such, discussion is kept to a minimum. This book is designed for practice teachers and also their trainers and mentors, so ideas for activities and exercises are included. These can be done, as self-development exercises, independently by practice teachers, or with their mentors. The exercises and role-play ideas are ideally for use with a group of practice teachers.

The idea for this book developed out of a Masters dissertation on the support and training needs of practice teachers, when working with failing students. It attempts to address some of the gaps practice teachers identified in their preparation for this task.

The focus of this book is practice teachers who are 'singletons' and as such are on site, within the placement, and assume the entire responsibility for it. It is not therefore designed specifically for workplace supervisors and 'long arm' practice teachers, nor for work-based placements found more usually on part-time or employment-based DipSW programmes. Although there will be some relevance, these kinds of practice teaching arrangements can produce situations outside the scope of this book.

Similarly, we are aware that some placements fail to provide a positive learning environment for students. This can reflect poor or under-resourced practice teaching. These situations are not the focus of this book. For its purpose, we are addressing issues where the practice teaching is adequate and the area which is of concern, is realistically the student's practice.

Throughout this book, the word 'failure' is used quite deliberately. Technically, the phrase 'not yet competent' or 'not yet ready to practice' used by some DipSW programmes is correct. However, the term 'failure' seems more appropriate to the realities of DipSW programmes, where students cannot present themselves automatically for reassessment, but have to be granted a repeat placement by an Assessment Board. Certainly as regards the real experience of the student and others involved in the placement, any other word but failure seems euphemistic and denies the emotional reality for students, their trainers and the words they use to describe it.

The assumption throughout this book is that the maintenance of high standards in practice learning are essential in professional social work training. We consider that any student who seeks a professional qualification is tacitly accepting the professional nature of social work, as is any practice teacher who selects to train them. This requires practice teachers to assess thoroughly the practice competence of students and to fail them if necessary. In the last resort, if there is any conflict between service users' rights and students' needs, then the former must prevail. Students should be prepared for this, if they wish to join a profession which is privileged to work with, and be accountable to some highly vulnerable people.

The pronoun 'she' will be used when referring to practice teachers and 'he' when referring to students. Scenarios and case studies used in this book are fictitious but they reflect situations that practice teachers could realistically encounter, albeit on an occasional basis.

1 A review of social work training

Dilemmas for practice teachers

The low failure rate of social work students on qualifying courses, which, in 1993, according to unpublished findings by the Central Council for Education and Training in Social Work was two per cent, has been recognised since the 1980s, and is well documented (Brandon and Davies 1979; Symans 1980). Studies during this period regarded the low failure rate as evidence of low standards in student selection and poor assessment, which led to students passing who should not. The 1980s saw developments in social work training which were influenced by several factors:

- There was a growing interest, led by CCETSW, in the assessment of social work students which sprang from increased disenchantment with traditional training methods
- Employers were questioning the contemporary relevance of the Certificate of Qualification in Social Work (CQSW) in light of new patterns of service delivery, changing social need and legislation
- Concerns were raised by child abuse cases, such as the case of Jasmine Beckford where a public enquiry attacked slack standards in social work training.

All these factors dovetailed with government pressure on CCETSW to identify the profession's knowledge and skills component and make the social work activity more explicit.

Changes in the 1980s

During the 1980s, successive governments were enthusiastic about any mechanisms in education and training processes which could achieve greater specificity, with competence broken down into smaller parts, to make training relevant to the needs of employers. This applied to the wide range of vocational qualifications in existence and these innovations, underpinned by Thatcherism, accompanied the extension of market principles to higher and further education.

Government agendas were reflected in the White Paper *Employment for the 1990s*, which aimed to place competence-based systems of learning and assessment centre stage, in promoting a skilled workforce, validated by occupational standards of excellence. The strategic coordination of this training policy was not left to professional bodies entirely. The government set up the National Council for Vocational Qualifications (NCVQ) in 1986, vested with establishing a national system of vocational qualifications which would eventually incorporate professional qualifications. It represented a response to the view that the United Kingdom lagged behind in vocational training and needed an employer-led, workplace-based training system. Its rapid growth meant increasing influence over various training bodies, reinforced by enthusiastic government support, which insisted that publicly funded courses adopted competence structures.

Consistent with this, and faced with a plethora of interest in social work and its education, CCETSW produced key policy documents, which signified a turning point in qualifying training. Paper 30 (1991, rev. 1995) identified a statement of knowledge, skills and values needed for competent social work practice and established a new DipSW course. This introduced a competence-based approach which reflected a shift to an outcomes-led assessment system. It also reflected CCETSW's agreement to establish a progressive framework of education and training, and secure social work education eventually within the continuum of NCVQ.

In 1995, Paper 30 was revised in response to government pressure and CCETSW collaborated even more closely with NCVQ's Care Sector Consortium to produce occupational standards, based on functional analysis appropriate for DipSW holders. It attempted to answer criticisms of earlier attempts to introduce a competence-based system of social work training and to produce a more holistic approach.

Practice teaching prior to DipSW

CCETSW also introduced changes in practice teaching arrangements for the new DipSW course. Prior to the Seebohm report and the setting up of

Social Service Departments (SSDs) in the 1970s, the major training bodies relied on experienced and proven practice teachers, in their specialist field, to provide placements. The 1970 Local Authority Social Services Act saw many of them absorbed into managerial posts within the new departments, and no longer available for student training.

A proliferation of new and varied courses led to increased pressure for placements, but no readily available body of trained practice teachers. Prior to DipSW, all CCETSW required for practice teaching was two years' experience following qualification, and a short non-assessed practice teaching course. Practice teaching was unrewarded by status and money and therefore could be viewed not as an important function *per se*, but a stepping stone to promotion, often into supervisory functions, leading to a high turnover amongst practice teachers. CCETSW's (1989) study estimated a 50 per cent turnover, which reflected an inexperienced group of practice teachers, who undertook student supervision on an irregular basis and with their own training unintegrated.

The literature of the 1970s and 1980s reflected, amongst social work trainers, an increasing dissatisfaction with the limitations of the CQSW assessment model. The low failure rate was a focus for this dissatisfaction, but other concerns were that the assessment process was tutor-dominated. It was not unknown for practice teachers' fail recommendations to be overthrown by tutors, reflecting an almost supervisory approach towards practice teachers. Certainly practice teachers often felt not accepted as full partners and disempowered in awarding CQSWs, because the full machinery for this remained with the educational establishment, whose regulations governed the assessment process.

However the literature of this period indicated little dissatisfaction on the part of practice teachers with this situation. Instead a common theme, as identified by Davies (1979) and Morrell (1979) was that practice teachers preferred not to take the responsibility for failing students. They only wanted to own pass decisions, with the responsibility for failing students being taken by the educational establishment. It was therefore left to social work trainers and academics to express dissatisfaction with the low assessment standards and it was this group, prior to the commencement of DipSW, who advocated reforms to combat weak assessment methods. Some of the changes called for consisted of:

- A strengthening of the practice teacher role and responsibility, requiring a clear Pass/Fail decision, with a practice teacher's, rather than tutor's, identification of a borderline student
- The need for a first placement to be passed before proceeding to the second

- A panel to approve assessment reports with strong practice teacher representation as a means of reinforcing their input into practice assessment.

The low failure rate was explained by the assessment practices of CQSW courses (Brandon and Davies 1979; Curnock and Prais 1982; Kadushin 1976). Assessment has two components. The first is an ongoing learning process in which students' work is reviewed, with competence highlighted and weaknesses minimised. Learning is therefore emphasised, with feedback being a shared practice teacher/student task.

The second component is the assessment event, with a decision which cannot be shared. The CQSW focused practice teachers more on the teaching and enabling functions, with attention on the learning process, rather than assessment decisions. This focus reinforced practice teachers' reluctance to address failure and CQSW training reflected a tendency to pass students providing they gave no evidence of incompetence, rather than requiring them to demonstrate competence.

The social work profession was not alone during this period in expressing concerns about the competence of newly qualified recruits. Similar low rates were identified in other vocational training, such as doctors, lawyers and teachers. This was significantly different in occupations such as accountancy and dentistry which have higher failure rates, reflecting a concentration on technological skills which are more easily quantified and measured. The low failure rate and a tendency to give the benefit of the doubt to marginal students seemed therefore to relate to occupations involving interpersonal skills.

Reformers advocated an increased focus on the assessment event, with CCETSW being pressed to attempt a specific knowledge and skills definition with explicit practice-evidenced criteria.

Practice teaching and assessment of students practice for DipSW

CCETSW's response introduced changes in practice teaching arrangements for the new DipSW course. Paper 26.3 (1989) and Paper 30 (1991, revised 1995) established guidelines/requirements for agencies and practice teachers, which reflected an unprecedented thrust towards the training and specialisation of this function. This initiative was designed to produce a body of trained and experienced practice teachers, with the ultimate objective that all DipSW students receive placements in an approved agency and be supervised by an accredited practice teacher.

These documents indicate several shifts of emphasis:

- The introduction of a competence-based system of assessment, is designed to require programmes to be more vigorous in the assessment of students' competence to practice
- Practice placements become 50 per cent of the course, with an attendance requirement
- The first placement must be passed before progression to the second.

These CCETSW (1991) initiatives formalised the use of the term 'practice teacher', as opposed to that of the traditional student supervisor. They become the person: 'responsible for undertaking the formal assessment of students' practice'.

Practice teachers therefore became responsible for making a full assessment decision, empowered to adopt a partnership role with tutors and with accountability to the Assessment Board. This includes:

- Providing the student with evaluative feedback on tasks
- Making a written report on progress in prescribed areas
- A clear requirement on practice teachers to undertake direct observation of practice.

This represents an attempt to provide more stringent assessment processes, to offset low failure rates. Within the supervisory function the task of assessment is, if anything, given more weight than the traditional ones of support and education. It therefore emphasises the practice teachers' accountability to the profession, and their gate-keeper function to ensure the validity of the license to practice awarded to the social work profession's new recruits.

These changes however were introduced against a background of low failure rates in placements, practice teacher reluctance to take assessment responsibility, and with accreditation and training requirements only just beginning. Additionally, the group of practice teachers available for the new DipSW courses were themselves trained and passed within this low failure culture. They were also rooted in a specific educational philosophy, yet required to adapt to an unfamiliar competence-based assessment framework, set against the background of an unresolved academic/vocational debate in the profession, regarding the validity of competence-based assessment versus traditional methods. This was accompanied by some dissatisfaction with the competence-based model and its appropriateness for higher education.

This is the background, therefore, against which practice teachers face the assessment of students, of which the failing process is an integral and complex part. They are expected to implement these changes, as well as cope with the relentless pressure to provide student placements. It is small wonder, therefore, that practice teachers find the enhancement of their assessment function difficult, and the prospect of failing students, which invites a closer scrutiny of their practice, daunting. The purpose of this book is to try and make this process more manageable.

2 Practice teaching and the DipSW assessment process

The report is written – what happens then?

Practice teachers may not always be familiar with the procedures which are implemented once their assessment report is completed. Failing a student focuses attention on the placement, and the practice teacher's report is inevitably highlighted. A knowledge of assessment procedures is therefore particularly needed when failing a student. Uncertainty as to what happens to the report once it has been sent to the student's university, can be an additional pressure when undertaking this complex process.

Failure often precipitates a crisis for the student and placement. Any difficulty in dealing with this can be aggravated if practice teachers only have a vague awareness of what the procedures are, and have to take time to search out the information. Familiarity with procedures therefore provides the necessary structure to the failing process. It needs to be part of practice teaching training, addressed at Learning Agreement meetings and placement briefing workshops, so it is an everyday part of a practice teacher's repertoire.

Process of assessment

Once a practice teacher completes her report and sends it to the university, a fairly lengthy process is set in train. To the practice teacher it can sometimes seem as though the outcome of her efforts enters a vacuum and she may have many queries:

- What happens next?
- What is expected of the practice teacher when a student fails?

- Is the report good enough?
- How does she find out the final outcome?
- What will happen to the student?

Most DipSW programmes request practice teachers, at the interim evaluation stage, to 'flag' up any student who is considered unlikely to be competent by the end of the placement. This does not of course then require a practice teacher to subsequently go on and fail a student, if he makes the necessary progress.

At any stage the student's tutor should be notified if problems occur. The tutor's role is to try and assist in the resolution of difficulties. The tutor is in partnership with the practice teacher, but the latter makes the pass/fail recommendation. The practice teacher is accountable for her assessment decision only to the Assessment Board which gives her a high degree of autonomy.

Occasionally placements 'break down' before the assessment process is complete. A student may request another placement, although any agency asked to provide an alternative will expect sound reasons. Similarly a practice teacher or tutor may terminate a placement. If this occurs a practice teacher can often be asked to complete a report on the student's progress up to this point.

Once a placement is complete, the practice teacher prepares an assessment report which includes a recommendation regarding pass or fail, in line with the terminology of the particular programme. The student should have the chance to read and sign it as well as to make comment on it. Ideally the student should be involved in both the assessment process and the report writing. Many reports also include a placement evaluation section for the student, practice teacher and tutor to complete.

Each programme must have a system for handling potentially failing students; outlined below is a diagrammatic summary of one such process (Fig. 2.1).

Practice Assessment Panel (PAP)

Once the report is prepared it is forwarded to the university concerned and then becomes a component in the process connected with the Practice Assessment Panel. All DipSW programmes must, in line with CCETSW (1995) guidelines, have a PAP: 'Programmes must have mechanisms to co-ordinate and monitor the standards of consistency of practice learning and assessment arrangements.'

The PAP therefore provides one method by which agencies can meet the procedures laid down by CCETSW regulations for the Approval of Agen-

INTERIM EVALUATION
Student is identified as failing

3-WAY MEETING
Student, practice teacher and tutor

Does college require
a second opinion

YES   NO

Remedial action plan formulated
Practice Assessment Panel is involved at this stage

PRACTICE TEACHER'S REPORT TO UNIVERSITY
Fail recommendation

PRACTICE ASSESSMENT PANEL
Requests additional evidence if necessary

REPORTS TO EXTERNAL EXAMINER

INFORMAL MEETING
Practice teacher, tutor and external examiners

ASSESSMENT BOARD → Pass
                    Fail decision
                    Refer

Most programmes will have a process whereby the student's 'voice' can be heard or represented at the Assessment Board stages.

Figure 2.1   Diagrammatic summary of one process for failing students
(adapted from the Nottingham Trent University DipSW programme
procedures)

cies, to ensure the quality of practice teaching. PAPs consequently have a quality control function and are established to:

- Monitor reports and make recommendations to the Assessment Board
- Identify marginal and disputed cases
- Assess the sufficiency, adequacy of the assessment evidence and the appropriateness of the recommendations
- Ensure there is sufficient evidence based on direct observation of a student's practice
- Identify training needs for practice teachers and give feedback to the agencies on the quality of the practice learning opportunities.

The PAP consists of both university staff and practice teachers, including representatives from both statutory and voluntary agencies connected with the specific DipSW programme. It can be chaired by agency representatives who are often practice teachers. It reports to the programme management and also the Assessment Board, and an external examiner may act as an adviser/consultant.

The Panel's function is to ensure the adequacy and sufficiency of practice teachers' reports. It cannot overturn a practice teacher's judgement but can request further evidence.

Usually, PAPs give feedback to all practice teachers on the quality of their reports. If this is not sent automatically, then a practice teacher should request it via the university tutor with whom she has worked on the placement. It is particularly useful to have this if a practice teacher is on award training, as it can be included in the portfolio she has to submit for award assessment. It can provide additional, objective feedback and evidence of her assessment and report writing skills. Box 2.1 at the end of this chapter gives a sample of criteria against which one PAP appraises reports.

Panel members consider in detail all reports on students who have a fail recommendation and any disputed or marginal cases. Some PAPs invite practice teachers and students to attend their meeting to discuss recommendations more fully. Programmes can vary as to the process for giving students a 'voice' in the assessment when they are failing and programme handbooks should give details on this.

The reports on all potential fail students are sent to the external examiner who does have the power to disagree and overturn the recommendation, consistent with all the marking done by the programme's tutor staff. It is customary for the practice teacher to be asked to meet with the external examiner, sometimes informally, prior to the Assessment Board or, alternatively to attend the Board's meeting. Again, arrangements can vary from programme to programme. The final decision is taken by the Assessment Board and the practice teacher should certainly expect to be advised of the outcome.

The Assessment Board

The Assessment Board takes responsibility for all formal assessment decisions regarding the student's progression on the course and it awards the DipSW. If a student fails on placement only and has satisfied academic requirements, then a repeat placement in an alternative setting can be offered. Assessment Board membership includes:

- Representatives of university staff
- Representatives of those engaged in practice-based learning
- Chair(s) of the PAP
- External Examiners taken from the CCETSW-approved panel.

The Board is usually chaired by the university Head of Department and excludes any student representative who is a current student on a DipSW programme. In performing its functions, the Board's effectiveness depends on the material to which it has access. When considering the future on a programme where a student has failed a placement, the importance of the practice teacher's report cannot be underestimated and its quality contributes to a Board's members being able to judge a student's work fairly, with the best possible outcome being decided for the student.

The role of the external examiner

These are appointed from a CCETSW-approved panel and cannot be employees of any of the programmes providers. They have formal responsibilities to attend Assessment Boards, ensure assessment arrangements approved by the CCETSW have been carried out and assist programmes to maintain common minimal standards. In line with this, External Examiners sample assessment evidence and judgement, and examine evidence for marginal and borderline students.

Roberts (1996) summarises the role of the external examiner as being that of ensuring a student's work is judged fairly when considered by the Assessment Board. They therefore need to be distant from the concerns of other Board participants, particularly institutional issues and pressure on resources. Their function is to ensure the student's work is assessed on the basis of sufficient and properly presented evidence consistent with the regulations for a particular programme, with which they need to be cognisant. This means an external examiner can argue that a student's work falls below minimal standards, as well as asking for leniency. They are not there to act as a third marker but to ensure fair play, as an informed counter-balance to potential vested interests.

The second opinion practice teacher

When the DipSW programme was established there was a requirement that an independent assessment be undertaken by a second opinion practice teacher on the practice of any student who received a Fail recommendation from a first practice teacher. The revised CCETSW (1995) DipSW require-ments made this provision no longer mandatory. It is left to each pro-gramme to decide how to exercise this quality control function. In view of the resource implications involved in supplying second opinion practice teachers, many programmes do not now use them routinely, but reserve them for special situations, for example where there are concerns about oppression or conflict of opinion. Some programmes have discontinued their use entirely.

Arrangements therefore vary from programme to programme and they should be clarified at Learning Agreement stage, so that practice teachers know at the beginning of their placement the arrangements made by the programme from which they are accepting a student on placement.

The appeals procedure

Students have the right to appeal against any Board decision; the appeals procedure usually embodies the following principles:

- That the assessment procedures have not been properly carried out
- That the participant has further evidence relevant to the assessment which was not available when the assessment was carried out.

An expression of dissatisfaction/dislike regarding the decision is therefore not sufficient grounds for appeal. According to Roberts (1996), there are increasing pressures within academic establishments, due to cost and the poor publicity of a successful appeal, to avoid giving students the need to do this, by attempting to achieve good practice and get the decision right. The right to appeal is part of this process, and a practice teacher should recognise its function, and not allow talk of appeal to be used in a threaten-ing or controlling way.

Appeals are handled by an Academic Review group whose members do not include any person directly involved in the original assessment decision and if it decides an Appeal should be upheld, it will recommend that the Assessment board reconsiders its decision.

Mitigating circumstances

Most programmes allow students who fail placements to request consideration of any mitigating circumstances which might have impacted on their performance in placement. These are becoming more frequent, which is hardly unexpected in these days of student debt, self-funding and the need to work whilst on the course. These mitigating circumstances should be presented via the proper assessment procedures laid down by the programme. They can relate to the student's view of the learning opportunities provided by the placement and the learning environment. These factors usually do not become a part of the assessment of competence but may be a significant factor in determining whether a student should have another placement.

Complaints procedures

A student cannot appeal until the Assessment Board has reached its decision but it is not unknown for the procedures for complaint to be confused. All universities and agencies providing placements, as required by CCETSW (1995) should have clearly defined complaints procedures so that students can express dissatisfaction about the way they are treated. In fact, a student may invoke both appeal and complaint procedures. Roberts (1996) makes a useful distinction between the definitions of Appeal and Complaint: *an appeal* is a formal statement that an Assessment Board has made a decision which is procedurally improper, while *a complaint* is a formal statement that an individual or agency has failed to deliver something which the student was reasonably entitled to expect.

If a complaint is in process when an Assessment Board is considering the student's position, then this situation requires a statement of the outcome on the complaint so its potential effect on any decision can be considered. A Fail recommendation by a practice teacher is not grounds for complaint, within the Agency, but for appeal, if appropriate through the University's procedures; the Fail *decision* first must be confirmed by the Assessment Board. A student cannot appeal against a Fail *recommendation* from a practice teacher, as this is not ratified until it has gone through the university's assessment process.

It is helpful therefore to all involved in the placement if the practice teacher is clear on the distinction and acquaints herself with the broad outline of the appropriate complaints procedures, and can provide students with information as to how to access them.

Empowering a student to complain is not an easy process, particularly if the focus of the complaint is the practice teacher or the placement. However, the skills needed and process are not dissimilar to when service users complain, but students are often more empowered to do so. When students complain, they are in the position of colleagues rather than service users and present in the work setting whilst the complaint is being dealt with. A practice teacher is usually unaccustomed to dealing with complaints from colleagues within her work setting and to dealing with them in a training rather than a social work capacity. This can invoke tension for all involved.

The ability of a student to complain should hopefully be regarded as positive, and consistent with the social worker's need to challenge. Unfortunately often only students who are at risk of failure feel able to do this. Sometimes the complaint can reflect an unrealistic blaming attitude and failure to take responsibility for their own learning and mistakes. In other instances they, as well as students who are successful in their placements, may find issues and poor practice about which they wish to speak up. They should be able to do this and receive a response from an agency which is not defensive, but committed to promoting a good service, which includes owning failure and learning from poor practice. Much depends on the culture of the organisation as to whether a complaints process can be seen in this light. A practice teacher can have a key role in facilitating students' right to complain, and it is useful for them to think through some of the issues. Activity 2.1 addresses some of the issues raised during complaints procedures.

Activity 2.1   Identifying cause for complaint

Contents: self-development and discussion exercise
Resources: activity sheets and flipchart
Time needed: one hour

This exercise can be done independently, or ideally with a group of practice teachers. The first part should be done independently and ideas shared with a partner. The pairs should then discuss the student situations and list their ideas on paper for sharing with the whole group in discussion afterwards.

A.   Think of a situation where you have wanted to complain about something but did not do so. It can be work-related or in your personal life. In the box below, list why you did not complain:

In the box below, list three reasons why you wish that you had complained and three reasons why you are pleased you did not:

In the box below, list what would have helped you make the complaint:

B.   Think of a situation where a student might wish to complain. Describe what in your work setting would:

a)   Make it difficult for the student to complain
b)   Assist the student in making the complaint

Write a checklist of things you could do to overcome the factors which would prevent the student complaining.

C.   Consider the following situations.

a)   Your student complains behind your back to your line manager that you are not supervising him adequately, and that the work you are giving him is too difficult for a student. What would your reaction to this be? How would you want your student to deal with this?

b)   Your student tells you that he has been to a case conference in a residential unit which is managed by your agency and the occupancy level was above the permissible numbers. Your student obviously expects you to do something about this and to make a formal complaint. What would you do? What would you advise your student to do?

c)   Your student tells you that she has experienced racism at a meeting in a school. Colleagues from your own department were also present and did nothing to challenge this. Your student is vague about the content of the remarks but she obviously experienced racism emotionally. What do you do about this? What do you advise your student to do about this?

d)   Your student has a physical disability and uses a wheelchair. Your placement setting lacks the resources she needed. You intend to raise concerns about this with your agency. Your student asks you not to as it will probably mean the placement would not be offered again to students with a disability. What do you do?

Police Checks

These are usually mentioned at Learning Agreement Meetings, for confirmation that this check has been completed on the student. In fact the placement should not commence without their completion, in situations where they are required. If in any doubt as to the policy and procedure of their Agency, practice teachers should check with their training section. However it is useful if they are acquainted with the position generally regarding them, as these issues are sometimes not addressed in practice teacher training or programme briefing workshops.

Local authorities regard police checks as an important part of establishing the suitability of a person who will have 'substantial access to children'. Since 1986, Government guidelines (HOC(86)44, DES 4/86, LAC(86)10, WOC(86)28, revised 1988) have introduced access to police checks for local authorities. The information provided in the police response can be:

- No trace of the person on the details provided
- Full details including cautions and bindover orders
- Other relevant information, including factual information the police would be prepared to present as evidence in court or a decision not to prosecute where circumstances give cause for concern.

The practice of DipSW programmes

At DipSW selection stage, the information provided by the programme for applicants usually includes a statement to the effect that selection for social work is exempt from the provision of the Rehabilitation of Offenders Act, so all criminal convictions must be stated. Applicants are usually advised that a police check needs to be made for any previous convictions, to which they must consent in writing. Selection panels can also sometimes reinforce the position verbally with applicants at interview. It is worth noting, as it sometimes causes confusion for practice teachers, that applicants are not required to state whether there is a file open on them in a Social Services department or voluntary agency, if they have been a service user.

Some diversity can exist on the reference process, if a practice teacher works with a variety of programmes. Many will take up police checks on all students, before they commence the course, on the expectation that a student could be placed in a setting where they undertake unsupervised work with children. Others may not, but leave it to the placing agency to initiate if a student requests a placement in a child care setting. In all instances, this matter should have been addressed before a practice teacher is asked to commence a placement.

Most programmes also will take very seriously any student's failure to declare, and may advise that failure to disclose can lead to termination of studies, regardless of whether the offence itself would be disregarded by an agency. The programmes' concerns focus around the dishonesty and lack of integrity/understanding by a student that a failure to disclose can represent. Once an applicant makes a statement of convictions, programmes will give attention to confidentiality, for example, disclosures may be dealt with by the admissions tutor only and not revealed to the full selection panel.

Programmes rely on agencies with whom they are in partnership to initiate police checks. A record will not preclude a student from academic study in an educational setting, but may prevent him from being accepted for a placement, or being employed eventually as a social worker. If an agency will not accept a student for placement, it prevents the student, in view of the nature of DipSW training from being accepted onto the programme.

If a conviction is declared and/or confirmed by the police check, then several procedures operate:

- Designated member(s) of the programme– admissions tutor and/or programme leader – will be advised
- Designated personnel within the agency will decide whether a student will be offered a placement.

The criteria for this include:

- Whether the offence has been declared
- Nature of the offence – the safety of service users is paramount.

If the decision is made to allow the student a placement, then confidentiality is maintained and information concerning the offence is retained, usually with the people responsible for making the decision.

Practice teacher position regarding police checks

The reality for practice teachers is that they cannot assume a student placed with them has no criminal record, only that it has been declared, police-checked and their agency considers that, despite the offence, the student is still safe to practice. Invariably, for confidentiality and anti-discriminatory purposes, if a conviction has been disregarded by an agency, the details of the offence will not be shared with the practice teacher and placement managers. However, this does not mean that a student may not choose to share the information with a practice teacher, which is why an outline knowledge of the procedures and process involved can be helpful.

Disciplinary procedures

It is not unknown for a student who is on an employment-based course, or working for an agency during university holidays, to become the subject of disciplinary procedures and complex situations can arise:

- Suspension from work can include suspension from a placement
- Disciplinary investigation may not include suspension and a student can subsequently be exonerated.

The process however can be emotionally fraught and a student needs support from the practice teacher. She may only have the information that the student shares. Due to agency confidentiality practices, details about the cause of the disciplinary action may be difficult to obtain. These situations can cause anxiety for the practice teacher about whether the student's practice may be affected by the actions and the cause of it.

Such situations are unusual but it is helpful if a practice teacher is at least aware that they can occur. If they cause uncertainty, she should consult with the student's Line Manager and training section placement coordinator.

Accessing the information regarding procedures for failing placement

It is unrealistic for practice teachers to be fully informed of the details of all the procedures which can become operational in placements, particularly ones where a student is failing. It is however time well spent if practice teachers, as part of their placement preparation acquaint themselves with, and make readily accessible the range of procedures they might need to consult. The programme's handbooks and agency information packs should provide this information. It should also be included in the Learning Agreement meeting, as most will contain a section on what happens if problems occur.

This should be part of a process which places the reality of failure on the agenda, so it becomes an integral part of a placement from the start, with anxieties acknowledged and discussed and a clear idea by all as to how to proceed if failure seems likely. (Activities 2.2 and 2.3 provides an opportunity to practice situations which will involve use of these procedures.)

Should failure become a possibility, an awareness of the procedures and appropriate reference points can be an effective means of containing the immobilising anxiety which new practice teachers can experience when a placement reaches this crisis. Ignorance of procedures can be an additional pressure if a practice teacher's time is taken up worrying about what is the appropriate step to take in the assessment process. It can take up energy from the practice teacher which could instead be channelled into confident work with a student which enables development.

Procedures which may become operational in work with failing students include:

- Malpractice procedures
- Complaints procedures
- Appeals procedures
- Placement termination procedures.

Exercise 2.1   Becoming familiar with procedures

Content: role play
Resources: facilitators, prepared cards, video (optional)
Time needed: one and a half hours

A.   This exercise is designed to enable the practice teacher to:

- Become familiar with Assessment Board procedures
- Focus on situations pertinent to failing students, which are not a regular part of all placements
- Develop skills in managing an assessment situation which is specific to failing students.

This role play is best done with a group of practice teachers, divided into small groups:

- External Examiners (2)
- Tutor (1)
- Practice Teacher (1)
- Course Leader (1)
- Observer(s) – the rest of the group.

The participants are all given some information about a student and practice teacher, while additional information about the other roles is given only to the person playing it. Variations are possible with this exercise. For example it may be used with a video, or role-played with a minimum of two people playing practice teacher and external examiner. It can therefore be amended for use by two practice teachers who are 'pairing' for mutual support or by a practice teacher and a mentor.

Participants are asked to enact a meeting which has been requested by the external examiners. This is an informal meeting, preliminary to the Assessment Board later in the day. The purpose is to consider the practice teacher's Fail recommendation and whether the Assessment Board should be asked to grant the student a repeat placement. This meeting is enacted for about 25–30 minutes, after which the participants should reach a decision. The external examiners are responsible for chairing the meeting and making the final decision. This scenario can be changed and real-life experiences amongst those present could be substituted.

Information given to the whole group

Student is a white male in his 40s with a background in residential social work. His first placement was in a day centre for children with a practice teacher who was taking a first student. He passed this first placement. His second placement was in an area office adult services team which he failed. The areas of competence which caused concern were recording, time management and his oppressive communication with colleagues and service users.

Practice Teacher

The practice teacher is female, experienced and has recently completed award training. She failed the student after much deliberation. He had strengths, but his attitudes to colleagues and service users remained oppressive. Feedback from colleagues reinforced this view although it was difficult to evidence. Video evidence from a training session with a group of volunteers was used in the assessment and feedback. The student interrupted the volunteers consistently and tried to dominate the female facilitator with whom he was co-working, and his body language was oppressive. He proved resistant to feedback. The practice teacher has written a clear, well-evidenced report. The student added comments challenging the decision and stating that he could not show his real capabilities because he found his practice teacher oppressive and felt uneasy performing on video. The practice teacher has not before met with external examiners and is quite anxious about the process. She feels her practice is on the line, not the students.

Information given about the role

External examiners

1. A black female, with extensive experience as an external examiner. She is a university lecturer on a DipSW course.
2. A white female and new to the external role. An experienced practice teacher who recognises the stress of failing students and is sympathetic towards the practice teacher.

College tutor

A white female who has been tutor to the student throughout the course. She is the recipient of the student's distress and feelings about being unsupported in a predominantly female placement. Academically the student is competent although his practice study was referred.

Course leader

White male. Harassed and busy. He finds the Assessment Board a pressure and it comes at a very busy time of the academic year. He is aware that the student intends to appeal against a Fail.

After the role play the observers should comment on the process. The participants should then discuss the meeting, their feelings about it and have a general discussion about the assessment process and in particular the skills needed for this type of meeting, as well as their support and information needs.

Exercise 2.2   Further practice in procedures for failure

Content: discussion exercise
Resources: prepared cards and flipchart
Time needed: one hour

This discussion exercise is designed to:

● Develop knowledge about situations where it may be necessary to terminate a placement
● Develop skills in assessment situations specific to failing students
● Develop skills in using programme procedures in respect to failing students
● Increase awareness around issues connected with the procedures for failure.

This discussion exercise needs to take place with small groups of practice teachers who should be given the following scenario to read, discuss, and then share feedback. It can be adapted for a role play, of a meeting between practice teacher, tutor and student to provide an opportunity for a group of practice teachers to practice skills in handling confrontation.

Scenario

The student is male and on a final placement in a child care team. His practice teacher is female and inexperienced as a practice teacher. The student initially did not want this placement but he was told by his university that it was the only one available, so he had no choice. He has been unmotivated throughout. His first placement indicated no difficulty and his academic work is adequate. At interim stage of the placement he was identified as behind in several of the competences. They were 'not assessed' because he had undertaken insufficient practice. He regularly had reasons why cases allocated to him were unsuitable for a student. The student at the interim review challenged his practice teacher's experience and abilities to select suitable work for him. He had also taken several days away from the placement because of difficulties with transport and family problems.

The tutor made an additional visit two-thirds through the placement to review progress. At this meeting another issue was pertinent, as the student had removed from the office without permission case files he needed for reference, whilst working on his university-assigned practice study. The student insisted his practice teacher had said he could have the files and knew where they were. She challenged this, as it was not true. The student's response implied that she was lying.

Discussion pointers

- What should the practice teacher do?
- What should the tutor do?
- Who could be called into assist with this problem?
- Which programme/agency policies and procedures might apply?
- What do you think a likely outcome to this situation would be?
- Any other ideas/suggestions about this situation?

Box 2.1   A sample Practice Assessment Panel assessment report

PRACTICE ASSESSMENT PANEL

ASSESSMENT OF PRACTICE TEACHER REPORT

Practice Teacher:...

Student:..

a) Evidence of student's competence or lack of competence

Sections demonstrated/Not demonstrated

Comments:

b) Evidence of values (CCETSW Values statement)

Sections demonstrated/Not demonstrated

Comments:

c) Legal Awareness

Sections demonstrated/Not demonstrated

Comments:

d) Have 3 Direct Observations been made and clearly described? Yes/No

Comments:

e) Is the report legible and clear with appropriate use of language.? Yes/No

Any additional remarks:

Panel Member..

Workbase...

Tel. No..

(taken from Nottingham Trent University DipSW Programme 1998)

3 Assessment of failure

DipSW assessment – what is needed?

When working with any student, a practice teacher needs to be clear on what assessment involves. The DipSW, as already outlined in the section of this book which covers the background to practice teaching, places greater emphasis on assessment. The primary task is on the need for the student to provide evidence of competent practice, to the point that mitigating factors, such as student difficulties or inadequate practice learning opportunities, become secondary.

Practice teacher skills are now stretched more fully in assessment with all DipSW students, but never more so than when failing a student. A sound knowledge of the assessment framework and requirements is therefore needed. An effective starting point for this can be the recognition of the tensions which can be involved in the assessment process.

Constraints and dilemmas in assessment

There is a distinction between creating learning opportunities and the assessment of competence. Ideally, the two dovetail, and the former produces competent performance by a student. However, tension can occur when a student is unable to practice at a satisfactory level, despite the opportunity to do so. Similarly, constraints arise if a student becomes so inhibited by the fact that his practice is being assessed, that his learning is impoverished because he feels unable to take the risk of making the mistakes sometimes necessary for development. A prescribed view of good practice, with expectations regarding the standard of a student's performance curtails freedom in this area.

Similar tensions are found around a competence-based assessment model which focuses on outcomes rather than the learning process. Such a model reflects the adoption of the NVQ assessment framework into professional and higher education. This change has engendered an unresolved debate regarding its appropriateness. It is advisable for practice teachers to be aware of this. It sets their assessment work into context, as does also the knowledge of the change in educational thinking underpinning the assessment model they now operate, which in some instances may be different from the educational climate in which they trained themselves.

Critique of competence-based assessment

Confident assessors need to be at ease with their framework. This is not facilitated in social work training by the conflict surrounding the validity of competence-based assessment versus traditional methods, as to which are more reliable, valid, even superior. Within this debate an issue of relevance to social work education is whether a competence-based framework can be applied to the complexities and values of professional qualifications.

The social work literature reflects unease and unfamiliarity with the competence-based model. A prevailing argument is that social work training is more appropriately provided by an educational approach, which develops learning and reflective skills, as the profession has social interaction and subjectivity as a basis of practice. Problems are identified by Powells and Powells (1994) in moving to a skills based, objective assessment, as it does not respond to the evaluation of students learning needs. Instead these are prescribed and obscured by a narrow concept of competence based on immediate job requirements.

It has been argued that an emphasis on directly observing practice, to provide more accurate verification of behavioural outcomes, ignores inference and claims a false objectivity in assessment. Callendar et al. (1992) in their work on the acceptance of the competence-based model found general resistance in the care sector from professional groups – the NVQ model was regarded as a threat to professionalism and lacking in academic vigour. They concluded that competence-based terminology and concepts led to difficulties, as assessors became mystified with their task and overwhelmed with the paperwork.

Professional resistance to the introduction of competence-based assessment is founded on a criticism of its theoretical underpinning, as represented by Ashworth and Saxton (1990), Hodgkinson (1992) and Barnett (1994). A vigorous opponent of competence assessment, Marshall (1991) attacks the functional and behavioural perspectives underpinning the NVQ competence-based model. Both these theoretical approaches were popular in the late 1960s and 1970s and in the educational arena their goal was to identify what tasks individuals would ultimately be able to do. This approach is considered unsuitable for extension to higher education and only appropriate for a basic level of skills acquisition. Functional analysis compiles a competency statement after an analysis of employment functions and does not allow for unexpected responses, such as imagination.

Many critics are united by their scepticism rather than a common theoretical base. In social work education this contrasts with well-established traditions, based on Knowles' principles of andragogy (1984) which places emphasis on learning and understanding. This can create tension for social work trainers who are schooled in a tradition which ostensibly conflicts with the emphasis on behaviour of the competence approach.

Views in this debate are polarised, with an emergent group of advocates for the competence-based assessment model, and its potential for adaptation to become an effective one for professional qualifications. Jessup (1991) in particular confronts concern amongst educators as to whether the competence-based model can assess all aspects of learning. He is firmly rooted in the benefits of competence-based assessment. Although he concedes its unfamiliarity and terminology are a cause of tension amongst assessors, all other difficulties are comparable with those in all assessment methods, including traditional ones.

Jessup supports competence assessment as an appropriate, if not desirable method for all occupational and professional qualifications. Similarly a range of opinion, including Mitchell (1993) and Hager et al. (1994), conclude that concerns around the competence-based assessment model reflects its newness, and that frameworks can be developed to cover assessment requirements for professional qualifications. Any required learning can be encapsulated in outcomes statements and criteria set to judge them, and a small number of units can address the more complex performance needed, including values. Proponents of the model cite the Anglian University Assets Programme which uses core values and ethics performance. It represents a project designed to formulate an honours degree curriculum within the context of social work education, based on the educational philosophy of the NCVQ.

O'Hagan (1996) consolidates many of these arguments in his critique of the revised Paper 30 and advocates that it counters and accommodates many of the attacks on competence-led social work training. He argues that DipSW Partnerships should not be able to re-create the impression of a tickbox exercise, as the emphasis now is on the need for knowledge, values and skills to underpin competence, in a way which is pervasive and requires a holistic approach.

The pros and cons of competency assessment can be summarised thus:

CONS	PROS
Reductionist – a technicist approach to education, defining knowledge in light of bureaucratic needs.	Integrates assessment into learning process, so it takes a more significant role.
Combines traditional and progressive forms of vocationalism uneasily as students are expected to take control of their own learning but competencies are prescribed without consultation.	Supplements gaps in traditional methods. Emphasises effective performance. Leads to clear, overt assessment criteria.
Knowledge and understanding are subservient to performance. It is a compartmentalised system which is employer and organisation dominated.	Frameworks can be developed to cover assessment requirements of professional qualifications.
Assessment is a tickbox exercise. Ignores the holistic and dynamic complexity of social work. The sum is more than the parts and a technically competent student may still be unsatisfactory.	Values assessment presents challenges in any assessment system; a well-constructed framework can facilitate the best method of assessing values.
Assessment of job-specific performance understates knowledge and understanding with insufficient development of critical thinking about work context, purpose and values.	Assessment decisions are more reliable and evidenced, providing more guidelines for the subjective part of assessment.
Emphasises the individual student and obscures the agency setting contribution to worker (in)competence.	Stimulates work-based learning in ways which are imaginative and improves the workbase.

Whatever the stance taken on wider issues, a competence-based assessment model creates tension in assessment when transferred to full-time, non-employment-based DipSW courses. Time constraints are imposed on the assessment of social work students who are inducted for short periods into placement settings. NVQs, on which the DipSW competence-based assessment framework is modelled, is for regular employees. Within the NVQ setting therefore, candidates are not failed, but they can ask for reassessment, after a period of consolidation and further practice within their current job. This process is not viable for full-time DipSW students who have time-limited placements in which to demonstrate competence. If assessed as incompetent, the placement ends, and the student cannot re-present himself for assessment, at a later stage, in the same placement setting. An opportunity to resit the placement depends on an Assessment Board granting it.

The reality for practice teachers therefore is that however much they focus on promoting learning and development, their assessment function imposes time limitations on this, and in all placements the assessment decision must be made. In a Fail situation the decision has far-reaching implications for the student and the assessment component of practice teaching assumes paramount importance.

DipSW assessment function

CCETSW (1991, revised 1995) guidelines are clear as to the definition of assessment within DipSW. It occurs 'at any point where a Pass/Fail judgement has to be made on the basis of the student's performance. Evaluation is a continuous process designed to give feedback which enables the student to improve performance ... all evaluation should lead towards assessment of competence.'

Assessment therefore involves deciding on the value of a student's practice and whether its level of competence is sufficient. This task involves making subjective judgements, and therefore presents challenges on all placements whenever the Pass or Fail decision has to be made.

The Fail decision – grasping the nettle

When a practice teacher is asked to offer a placement, the student may already be identified as likely to fail. Indeed a student may have failed a first placement and be on a repeat.

Often, however, the likelihood of failure has not been identified. As the placement progresses, doubts about the student's competence can arise and create complex assessment decisions. Sometimes the decision is straightforward, if the student practices in a blatantly incompetent way, or the placement is terminated. However, many students are borderline and the decision is less clear, so considerable assessment skills are needed, involving judgement and self-knowledge. A practice teacher also needs to be confident about and have clear reasons for any assessment but particularly fail ones.

In respect to first-placement students, who are often placed with beginner practice teachers, it can be tempting to give the benefit of the doubt to the student on the expectation that, as long as some progress is made, it is sufficient just to identify areas where practice is barely adequate for improvement in the second. This approach can be unhelpful to all concerned and not least the student, as the longer the failing process takes, the more difficult and demoralising it becomes, alongside the gradual building up of the personal and financial pressures which social work training can involve. The longer a Fail decision is delayed, the more difficult the failing process can become, producing a climate where it can be tempting to 'shuffle' students through whose practice is doubtful. It can therefore be better to grasp the nettle at this stage, as only in exceptional circumstances are students who fail on a first placement not allowed a repeat placement. Extra time for consolidation at this stage can often be more useful than at the end of the course.

The more a practice teacher understands and becomes familiar with the requirements of the DipSW assessment framework, the more the task of assessment becomes manageable. This particularly applies to failing students who often pose the contentious and difficult decisions. Out of fairness to them, and to gain the necessary confidence to work with students, practice teachers need therefore to be clear about the assessment framework within which they operate and what competence is.

Competence – what is it?

A plethora of opinion exists as to what competence is, which can make it difficult to formulate a clear and all-encompassing understanding of the concept. O'Hagan (1996) provides a useful outline of the origin of the word and available definitions, and identifies the NCVQ's model as the most comprehensive:

> Competence is a wide concept which embodies the ability to transfer skills and knowledge to new situations within an occupational area. It encompasses the organisation and planning of work, innovation and coping with non-routine activities. It includes those qualities of personal effectiveness that are required in the workplace to deal with co-workers, managers and customers. (NCVQ 1988)

CCETSW in the revised *Requirements and Regulations* (Paper 30) (1995) came up with a broader definition of competence as a 'wide concept embodying … a demonstration of knowledge, values and skills'. It designates six common social work tasks as core competences, which are broad enough to be viewed as areas of competence:

- Communicate and engage
- Promote and enable
- Assess and plan
- Intervene and provide services
- Work in organisations
- Develop professional competence.

DipSW practice assessment therefore outlines a competence as a statement of a specific ability, presented as a description of what the attainment of competent practice requires. It can be broken down into *practice* requirements which describe what a student would be able to understand and know, and *evidence* requirements which provide concrete examples of the ability needed to prove competence.

Paper 30's approach is holistic inasmuch as it stipulates that the core competences can only be valid if underpinned by the application of knowledge, values and skills. Each student must also meet a *values* requirement and a *knowledge* requirement.

These requirements are linked to each core competence so that values and knowledge are integral to competent practice, and the evidence must be drawn from the specific practice undertaken by the student. An understanding of legislation is also given clear emphasis, as is the ability to reflect upon and critically analyse practice as well as to transfer knowledge skills and values. The same competences apply to both first and second placements as do the values requirements although they may vary for knowledge. There are however variations regarding placements:

- The first placement is 50 days' duration and assesses basic competence
- The second lasts for 80 days and can offer particular or generic pathways.

In both placements, students must demonstrate that they have met the practice requirements of core competence 'Assess and Plan' by working with service users who have significantly different needs and circumstances.

All DipSW programmes will give specific guidance on assessment which can be found in practice teacher handbooks. A practice teacher needs therefore to familiarise herself the interpretation of the CCETSW guidelines which the student's particular programme has made. This enables a practice teacher to be clear on the assessment task.

The Assessment task

In accordance with CCETSW guidelines, the assessment task judges a student's performance by criteria prescribed by the Council. The practice teacher is expected to assess the student's supervised practice, which must be integrated and underpinned by core values; however, CCETSW leaves it to each individual programme as to how this is done.

Assessment is an ongoing and formative process, which is ultimately consolidated in a summative final assessment decision. It is therefore a process which occurs throughout the placement, and is never confined to just one specific formal assessment event. Doel et al. (1996) draw the distinction between 'total assessment', when all the student's work is taken for assessment at agreed times, and 'sampling', where particular examples are taken for assessment. They make the point that in practice all assessment is sampled as it is impossible to include all the student's work in total assessment and the distinction is whether the sample is implicit or explicit, that is, whether it is *ad hoc* or planned.

Doel argues that sample assessment can be fairer to the student, as it is planned and timed so the student knows which aspect of practice will be assessed at which times. This argument is convincing, although it needs the recognition from practice teachers that assessment and feedback is ongoing and any practice can, if necessary, be judged. This is particularly important when working with failing students who can produce atypical situations. Professional accountability and the need to protect service users mean students cannot be given the impression that their work is only assessed on particular occasions and they can behave as they wish on others. In the event of highly incompetent practice or malpractice, a practice teacher needs to intervene and to include this in her assessment decision.

The assessment task in placements is on whether the student can function according to professional standards and become a social worker. This can run counter to the educational climate against which both students and their tutors operate, which initially can cause confusion and conflict. Often, as noted by Phillips (1996) the university climate emphasises promoting academic success and keeping students in the system, by making awards at the appropriate level of ability, and reducing the prospect of failure through the facility of multiple attempts. This is often not the climate in the workplace and it is a tension against which practice teachers have to operate when completing their assessment in the employer-led environment.

Within social work training there is a long-standing debate as to whether training can change attitudes and values. The DipSW assessment model approach is that the assessment task should deal with student behaviour. If a student's values and attitudes produce incompetent performance, then this is the focus and the student should fail.

Box 3.1   Outline for recording a practice teaching session

1.   Date, venue, duration of session

2.   Agenda items discussed

3.   Content of session – review work covered during the week

   ● Student activities, for example, clients seen, meetings attended
   ● Student records discussed, if any
   ● Direct observation undertaken, if any – feedback noted
   ● Contact with other agencies – networking undertaken
   ● Discussion of log, diary, case studies, etc.
   ● Discussion of any exercises completed
   ● Discussion of evidence for competencies.

4.   Planning future work

   ● Plans for clients
   ● Areas where student has difficulties
   ● Practical issues
   ● Competences not addressed or evidence still to be provided.

5.   Practice teacher's comments – student's development in terms of

   ● Educational issues, that is, barriers to knowledge
   ● Anti-oppressive issues
   ● Linking theory to practice
   ● Competence attainment – record of evidence already provided and reflection on areas where the student is failing to do so.

(adapted from Danbury 1994)

When undertaking the assessment task competence checklists can initially seem daunting. The process becomes more manageable if time is taken at the start of the placement to do the following tasks:

- Read through the assessment requirements and the programme's practice curriculum at the start of the placement, so they become reasonably familiar. A practice teacher should insist that she receives these at pre-placement stage and in advance of the placement starting
- Select work for the student which will allow their assessment to be undertaken. One major piece of practice can often allow a student to show ability or otherwise in several competences
- Consider well in advance if there will be any difficulty in accessing the necessary practice opportunities for a student in a placement setting, so that alternatives can if necessary be found in another workplace, or strategies devised which do not require direct practice
- Manage the assessment of competence. A practice teacher needs to consider how to organise the competence assessment so as not to dominate the practice tutorial, nor is it left until too late in the placement. It is best to integrate assessment into each supervision agenda and record the evidence for competences regularly throughout the placement. A useful discipline, which often saves time in the long run is for a practice teacher to record notes on the practice teaching session which integrate the attainment of competence. This can incorporate the agenda used and notes shared with the student.

Creating an effective environment for assessment

The assessment task requires assessment skills on the part of a practice teacher. Confidence and competence in this area is important in all placements, but never more so than when failing a student. It also needs the creation of a fair and constructive assessment environment. This can be achieved by a variety of methods:

- Involve the student in the choice of assessment methods and evaluate those selected at stages throughout the placement
- Take the student's learning style into account. For example, a reflective student may feel more able to evaluate his practice by a log or diary than impromptu discussion. An activist may prefer to video his practice or develop it by role play in practice teaching sessions
- Ensure the student knows the competences on which he is being assessed at a particular time, and the criteria which the practice teacher is using and the standard expected
- Accommodate where possible particular difficulties, such as dyslexia, visual or hearing impairment; use of English when it is not a first

language. Certain assessment methods may accommodate these more easily.

Involving the student in this way helps towards establishing an assessment climate in which the student feels safe, which is not easy when working with students who are failing. Assessment is the arena in which the practice teacher can feel most powerful and certainly be perceived as such by students. A failing student is particularly likely to experience the assessment process as oppressive and complain that he has not been able to show his true practice effectively. An effective climate for assessment can only be attempted therefore if a practice teacher can engage anti-oppressively with the student, and recognise and work with the power imbalance and the conflicts around it which underpin the supervisory relationship. No assessment can be neutral but bias can be regulated by its recognition, leading to open and honest self-reflection and consultation.

It is only fair therefore to the student, and a protection to the practice teacher that proper attention is given to issues around oppression, and effective contract work undertaken at the start of the placement. It is useful when undertaking this task if a practice teacher reflects on her own experience of being assessed and clarifies her thought/feelings about the process and her role as assessor:

- Address oppression issues at the start of the placement and how they might affect the relationship with the student and the placement
- Test out assumptions about self and the student (see Activity 3.1).

Activity 3.1   Where are you?

Contents: self-development exercise
Resources: copies of exercise
Time needed: one hour

This activity can be done independently or with a group of practice teachers working in pairs. It can be adapted for completion by practice teachers and their mentors, to explore their relationship preparatory to their work together on the award course. This activity is designed to encourage the recognition of differences which could form the basis of oppression, as well as ensuring that the power imbalance in the supervisory relationship is acknowledged. It can also assist with creating a safe assessment environment.

Practice teachers should complete this exercise independently first, with a view to doing it with their students to explore how differences might affect the supervisory relationship and assessment.

The practice teacher should complete this self-development exercise and discuss it with a partner if available.

Cultural background and identity

a)   List your idea of what your cultural background is.

b)   How do I view my cultural background?

1	2	3	4	5

Very positively   Very negatively

c)   How effective is my awareness level of other cultures?

1	2	3	4	5

Very high   Very low

How powerful/disempowered do I feel by culture/identity?

Plot your answers on the following on a scale of 1–5, with 1 being very powerful

Race	1	2	3	4	5
Age	1	2	3	4	5
Gender	1	2	3	4	5
Sexual orientation	1	2	3	4	5
Dis/Ability	1	2	3	4	5
Personality	1	2	3	4	5
Social background	1	2	3	4	5
Current social situation	1	2	3	4	5

Any other?					
Identify them	1	2	3	4	5

In which contexts do I feel

Most powerful?
Least powerful?

How do I respond to

Assessing others?
Being assessed?

Do this exercise with your student

Consider the differences between you.
Consider how the differences could be oppressive: by whom? How they could be resolved?

Other preparatory work sets the scene for effective assessment. The task requires the ability to identify the knowledge and skills involved in social work activity, to recognise when students are using them and to give feedback in these terms. This approach is familiar to a Certificate in Social Services (CSS) and DipSW-trained practice teacher, but is less familiar to those with CQSW backgrounds. The CCETSW delineation of the skills required in social work practice assists here. A practice teacher needs to be familiar with them.

They also need to assist students with the identification of learning needs and this should be based on the knowledge and skills students need to demonstrate competence as practitioners and not the areas of social work experience they wish to attain (see Activity 3.2).

Activity 3.2   Identifying knowledge and skills

Contents: task analysis and small group exercise
Resources: flipchart and paper, video equipment
Time needed: one and a half hours

This activity should be done with a group of practice teachers. The first section should be done with a partner. The second section needs practice teachers to work in small groups initially and then to share feedback with the whole group. For the purpose of this activity define a skill as the ability to perform a task and to use knowledge effectively when doing it.

Section A

- Reflect on your social work practice. Select one social work task you have completed recently
- Break this task down into the knowledge and skills you needed in order to complete it
- Identify and record the task under the following:

Skills   Knowledge   Attitudes

Section B

The group should make or use a prepared video recording of an interaction between a social worker and service users. The group should watch the video individually and record their ideas about the knowledge and skills being used. Ideas should be listed on a flipchart and discussed in a group.

A practice teacher who is new to supervising students may initially feel ill at ease with the assessment role and the responsibility it carries. She needs to be aware of her responses and feelings about this in order to develop confidence in assessing and engaging with the student in an open way through the process.

Activity 3.3   Self-development exercise on assessment

Contents: self-development exercise
Resources: copies of the exercise
Time needed: 40 minutes

This activity can be done independently or by two practice teachers or a practice teacher and mentor. It is designed to enable practice teachers to identify and share the personal feelings which can be aroused or transferred from previous experiences, by the need to assess and be assessed.

Think of a situation when you have been assessed

- How did you experience it?
- How did your assessor handle it?

Think of yourself as an assessor

- How comfortable are you with the role?
- How does it make you feel?
- What did you find most difficult about it?
- What do you find easiest about it?

Consider your assessment skills as a practice teacher or a social worker:

- What are your strengths?
- What are your weaknesses?

Identify your development areas:

- List the three main ones below:

Setting the ground rules for assessment

At an early stage in any placement, before assessment commences, it is a useful practice to undertake preparatory work with students on the supervisory function and to explore their previous experience of it and how assessment and appraisal fitted into this. Students' pre-course experience can vary considerably and some come on to DipSW courses with very limited experience of social work. An understanding of the supervisory models used in the practice teacher's work setting should therefore never be assumed, and students may bring very different agendas with them regarding supervision, based on previous educational experiences. For example:

- Students can perceive themselves as accountable to practice teachers only if they do something wrong, thus ascribing to supervisors an inspectorial role
- They regard the practice teacher as someone who will get them through the course
- They regard the practice teacher as someone who is a fount of knowledge who will direct, teach and 'spoonfeed' them, so they pass the placement
- They regard the practice teacher as a student colleague who will help them deal with the college tutor whom they regard as having an inspectorial role regarding the practice teacher and student

- They regard the university-based assignments as the important part of the course, with 'practical' work being easier and less important
- They regard the practice teacher as someone to help them with their college assignments and give study skills support.

The time taken to clarify and exchange ideas on supervision, the practice teacher's function and expectations as to how adults learn, can therefore be time well spent (see Activity 3.4). Ground rules can be established and differences identified regarding expectations should the practice teacher/ student relationship be tested with a fail assessment at a later stage. Sound contract work on what assessment is – its process and the methods to be used – can all help address the power imbalance. It can help establish groundrules for a situation where serious differences occur and a practice teacher may have to overrule the student. (Activity 3.5 at the end of this chapter outlines one suggested contract.)

Activity 3.4   Exchanging ideas on assessment

Contents: self development questionnaire
Resources: copies of questionnaire
Time needed: one hour

This activity can be done by practice teacher and student at the start of the placement as part of their contract work together. It can then be reviewed at stages throughout the placement. Both should complete it and share expectations regarding assessment. Any major discrepancies need discussion as to whether they can be resolved and how.

Practice teacher

I will expect my student to:

1. Take control of his/her own learning

1	2	3	4	5

    Constantly   Rarely

2. Identify the evidence of competence himself

1	2	3	4	5

    Always   Never

3. I will expect to use direct observation of my student's practice

1	2	3	4	5

Minimal times
the programme
  expects

Frequently

4. I will expect to use others in assessment

1	2	3	4	5

Constantly

Never

5. Whilst on the placement I will assess my student

1	2	3	4	5

At all times

On specific
occasions

6. If my student's practice seems unsatisfactory I will tell him/her

1	2	3	4	5

Immediately

When sure

7. If my student's practice seems unsatisfactory I will tell the tutor

1	2	3	4	5

Immediately

Not at all

8. After assessment I will give feedback

1	2	3	4	5

Immediately
afterwards

At the
placement end

9. I will involve my student in choice of assessment methods

1	2	3	4	5

Always

Never

Student

I will expect my practice teacher to:

1. Manage the placement

1	2	3	4	5

Teaching me at
 all times

Expecting me to
 direct my own
 learning

2. Find the evidence of my competence

1	2	3	4	5

Always

Involve me in
 this fully

3. To observe my practice directly

1	2	3	4	5

Never

Frequently

4. To use others in the assessment of my practice

1	2	3	4	5

Never

All the time

5. To assess my practice

1	2	3	4	5

Constantly

On specified
 occasions

6. If my practice seems unsatisfactory to tell me

1	2	3	4	5

Immediately

At the
placement end

7. If my practice seems unsatisfactory to tell the tutor

1	2	3	4	5

Immediately

When I agree

8.   After assessment to give me feedback
     1   2   3   4   5

- -

Immediately   Not at all

9.   Involve me in choice of assessment methods
     1   2   3   4   5

- -

I must agree   Never
  them

The competence-based assessment model was selected for DipSW out of unease at the low failure rate and a wish for more stringent assessment based on indicators, which it was hoped would make learning more measurable. This approach focuses on the outcomes not the process of learning. Consequently the student has not just to show progress but to have reached a level of competence. Whether or not this has been attained rests on the practice teacher's judgement of the evidence the student gives of his ability to practice.

In the history of practice teaching, regardless of what kind of assessment model is used, in all placements a point is reached when the assessment task is to decide whether a student is ready to pass the placement and qualify. At some point a practice teacher must make this decision and justify it.

Exercise 3.1   *Making a contract on assessment*

Content: contract assessment
Resources: self-development exercise
Time needed: one hour

This exercise is designed to be done with students – it lists ideas for establishing grounds on supervision and assessment.

A   *Purposes of supervision*

- Ask your student to consider and then record what he thinks are the main purposes of supervision and his expectations of you as a supervisee
- Do the same yourself
- Exchange the ideas you have both written down
- Discuss areas of similarity and difference
- Clarify how differences will be resolved and record the outcome.

B   *Aims for the placement*

- Ask your student to write down briefly what his aims are for the placement
- Do the same yourself and exchange aims
- Discuss areas of similarity and difference and record the outcome.

Note to practice teachers: The aims for the placement can be different from learning needs which link to skills and knowledge areas the student needs to develop in order to demonstrate competence. Placement aims can relate to areas such as whether the student wants to make maximum learning possible or just to pass the placement, both of which are valid as long as competence is demonstrated. Similarly placement aims may link to a specific career pathway the student wishes to pursue. Acknowledgement of mutual aims can clarify issues, reduce misunderstanding and guide the practice teacher on what learning opportunities the student needs.

C *Assessment methods*

- Identify with your student the assessment methods you will use
- Agree and record them.

Note to practice teachers: You need to clarify that direct observation of practice is required and that you reserve the right to use it more frequently than the programme's minimum requirements if necessary. Otherwise this exercise allows your student to discuss/agree with you on methods he would feel most at ease with and would suit his learning style. Take into account any special needs. You can reserve the right to insist on a certain assessment method if needed, with your reasons.

D *Power issues*

- Recognise the power imbalance in your relationship with your student
- Discuss and identify how you can attempt to redress it without denying your assessment responsibility.

E *Failure*

- Clarify your experience/position on this with your student
- Identify how you would deal with this, for example prompt feedback, no sudden surprises at the last minute, agree to allow time whenever possible for remedial action.

F *Confidentiality*

- Clarify boundaries on this
- Agree and record them, for example, no secrets are possible – malpractice, unprofessional or unethical issues cannot be kept confidential.

G *Contact with tutor*

- Identify situations where you may contact the tutor
- Identify situation where the student may do so
- Discuss and clarify expectations regarding telling each other first if the tutor is being called in regarding failure or a contentious matter, a disagreement, or a complaint.

4 The decision to fail

The need to make and evidence the decision

In all placements, there comes a time when a practice teacher must decide whether a student passes or fails. Indicators of failure can present at any stage of a placement, but they are often there from the start. For example, a student may commence a placement with difficulties and learning needs clearly identified in a previous placement. In other situations, a practice teacher may experience a gut feeling of unease, or colleagues may become concerned about the student's practice and give the alert. Alternatively a student may develop personal difficulties, which prevent attendance on placement or stop him resolving conflicting demands on his time. Sometimes a complaint may be made about a student's practice which may after investigation become an indicator of poor practice.

Whatever the reason for concern, once a student has been given a chance to practice, feedback, and time to learn and develop, a decision then has to be made as to whether his level of competence is sufficient. This decision also has to be evidenced.

Evidence collection

One reason for the introduction of the competence-based assessment model into DipSW was a wish for more stringent assessment. A practice teacher's job is to judge whether or not the student's performance is competent and to collect evidence to back up this decision. The emphasis is on the student being able to practice competently. The ability to simply make some progress is no longer sufficient as it sometimes was under CQSW. Practice teaching continues to encompass both support and learning but the DipSW approach also places greater emphasis on assessment. Inevitably the processes are interwoven but at some point the practice teacher must make and evidence the assessment decision.

Although failing a student is never a welcome task, the DipSW assessment model focuses a practice teacher more on the need to do so. It requires her to state explicit reasons for the assessment decision against specific indicators, so it becomes less easy to ignore poor practice and avoid making unpopular decisions by excessively giving the benefit of the doubt to a student. Similarly the need to provide evidence, and to observe a student's practice directly, requires practice teachers to confront situations when evidence is not available, and incompetence becomes highlighted.

Practice teachers must therefore be clear on the evidence they have to collate and the practice opportunities they have to provide for their students. The student's particular DipSW programme will provide details of the assessment required and the report/evidence needed. In some ways the DipSW assessment model and its focus on evidence makes the failing process easier:

- It is based on tangible, often factual evidence which is more measurable
- Evidence is available for scrutiny by others, so that a practice teacher's judgement can be validated
- The student knows the assessment criteria against which he is judged. He can therefore feel more empowered and assume some responsibility for providing the evidence
- A student is rarely incompetent in all areas of practice; the decision to fail can be less demoralising if some competence can be accredited
- The basis of the evidence is on knowledge, skills and values, so it is easier to make the failing process constructive. The focus is on a student's performance and behaviour, so he can be less likely to feel a failure as a person
- Some programmes require students to contribute evidence to the assessment report. This can be empowering and enables others to scrutinise the raw material on which the practice teacher is basing her judgement.

Clear evidence for the assessment decision is needed in all placements, but it is particularly essential when failing students:

- It is only fair to students, as it enables the assessment decision which is in their best interests to be made

- The report from a practice teacher who fails a student will inevitably be scrutinised by the programme's assessment process. A clear, well-evidenced report facilitates sound assessment, and the appeals process, if a student initiates this
- A fully substantiated, practice-linked decision forms a valid baseline for students who wish to appeal and provide additional evidence
- The need to give evidence for the decision provides students with some protection against an irresponsible decision to fail, reflecting a practice teacher's incompetence, bias or lack of placement resources. It assists in redressing the power imbalance.

A practice teacher who takes the step of failing a student usually feels strongly that he is not ready to practice as a qualified social worker. She has a responsibility to both the agency, as a potential employer, as well as to service users to substantiate this decision fully. She therefore needs to consider carefully the reasons for the failure and to collate the evidence for it, based on the student's practice.

Selection of work for a student

This is crucial in the assessment and evidence-gathering process. When selecting work therefore it is necessary to take the following considerations into account:

- Which competences a student will be able to demonstrate from undertaking a specific task
- The appropriateness of the work for the specific assessment method selected, such as direct observation or recording
- A variety of work to encompass all the evidence needed.

If a placement does not provide direct practice opportunities for a student to meet all competences, it may be necessary to arrange for a student to spend part of the placement in another work setting, or to use simulation exercises which will provide the student with the opportunity to demonstrate competence. Danbury (1994) outlines in detail the components of a good teaching case and refers to exercises which have been devised in the absence of suitable case materials.

Once work for a student is selected, there are many assessment methods which can be used to gather the necessary evidence of competence:

Direct evidence	*Reflective evidence*
Direct observation of the student's practice	Discussion
Consumer feedback	Supervision notes
Observation of others	Case studies
Video/audio recordings of live interviews	Recordings – diary, log, agency records
Exercises	Student's evaluation of
Simulations	learning

When gathering evidence, various aspects need consideration; the evidence must be:

- Valid – to cover a requirement of the practice curriculum and assess what is intended
- Sufficient – to justify the assessment decision
- Fair – to everyone involved
- Reliable – the evidence must be consistent, for example, different assessors should agree it,; the same method should produce the same outcome on different occasions
- Clear – comprehensible to all involved.

There are different kinds of evidence, so the method of assessment and the kind of evidence it will produce needs to be linked to the competence, for example whether it is a technical skill such as recording, or information-gathering, or one linked to values and skills. In many instances, areas of technical competence are easier to address and remedy as the evidence is more tangible.

The assessment task is often more complex when the unease arises from the student's values attitudes and interpersonal skills. Here the decision calls upon the practice teacher's professional judgement and confidence in assessment skills. All assessment methods rely, in the last resort, on some personal judgement and a practice teacher who is confident as an assessor needs to be comfortable with this reality.

Hayward (1979) argues that assessment involves accepting that human judgement can deal with a variety of ways of perceiving, interpreting and acting, particularly if set within a system that recognises it is imprecise and attempts to develop objective approaches. In her view, constant denigration of human judgement as imprecise, whilst ignoring its richness and breadth, is biased. Assessment therefore should aim to neutralise the least desirable effects of a subjective type of assessment, whilst its benefits are retained. Evans (1990) considers that DipSW assessment, with its delineation of competence and the indicators to be examined moves social work assessment towards this, but the individual assessor still makes the professional judgement of standard.

The unquantifiable, non-measurable nature of standard setting in social work competence challenges assessors to the utmost. Work with failing students tests ultimately the assessment framework and the skills of the practice teacher. Certain kinds of evidence can be best adapted to this process.

The validity of direct evidence

The assessment of failing students can often be best assisted by the following methods, which produce direct evidence of practice, particularly in the more complex and contentious areas:

- Direct observation
- Feedback from others
- Audio/video recording of a student's practice.

The advantages of direct observation in the context of failure is that once a student is aware that there is concern about his level of competence, a practice teacher may find him anxious, uncooperative and resistant to assessment of identified areas. Direct access to a student's performance and the requirement to observe it can reduce this avoidance, as it opens up the student's practice to scrutiny by the practice teacher and her placement colleagues. This can prove an essential protection for all involved in situations where students are not ready to practice as professionally qualified social workers.

Ideally, direct observation of practice is an invaluable learning/teaching tool. Unfortunately in a few situations a practice teacher may need to use it as a means of finding evidence to fail a student, thus adopting a monitoring, more inspectorial function, if the student is unable to progress, or recognise the need to do so. These instances, albeit infrequent, need to be recognised and managed as much as possible in all placements, when organising the process for directly accessing students' practice and gaining evidence for its competence.

Direct observation of students' practice

The CCETSW (1995) requirement for DipSW, is that direct observation of students' practice must take place a minimum of three times in each assessed placement; one observation session may be undertaken by a workplace supervisor or video recording. On two occasions on each placement the practice teacher must observe the student with service users, and one direct observation should normally occur before the mid-placement stage. The purposes of direct observation are educational but the CCETSW guidelines also clearly ascribe to it an assessment function.

Educational

The direct observation requirement is regarded as an integral part of the learning process, ideally following several stages. Initially, in line with the model advocated by Doel et al. (1996), the student should have the chance to observe the practice teacher and her colleagues' good practice, so he can question and challenge. The practice teacher is thereby making her practice open to scrutiny, in an environment where everyone is learning and she is not subjecting the student to a process she is not open to undergoing herself. The student can then move on to take a lead role with service users, whilst the practice teacher observes and gives feedback on his performance, level of competence and areas for development.

Assessment and monitoring

Direct observation also has a clear assessment function. This is to monitor and ensure the quality of service by students, and to assess and evidence the student's performance.

Direct observation within the context of failure can assume different dimensions. Ideally, it takes place within a positive learning environment, with an effective relationship between student and practice teacher, and the student being involved in the selection of assessment methods appropriate to his learning style. Often with failing students, where the outcome of teaching and learning is incompetent performance, then it becomes a main method for producing concrete evidence of a student's lack of skill.

Practice teacher–student relationships may deteriorate when a student realises there is a concern about his level of competence. This deterioration can be characterised by:

- Lack of trust
- High anxiety levels
- Avoidance of supervision sessions
- Lack of cooperation
- Resistance to exposing practice to scrutiny by others.

This is a difficult situation, but, unless the relationship breaks down completely and the placement terminates, then it needs to be managed. It is essential that the practice teacher recognises and accepts the student's distress, but she needs also to be firm about direct observation being a requirement, not an optional part of the assessment process. Indeed, more than the required minimal occasions may be necessary, as such observation can provide valid evidence of (in)competence.

Preparation and ground rules

Careful preparatory work with students on direct observation is essential in all placements but never more so than when working with failing students, whose anxiety is high. They may not always hear what is said and certainly not absorb information in handbooks. Exercise 4.1 at the end of this chapter provides an opportunity for practice teachers to role play and discuss preparation for direct observation.

Setting ground rules for direct observation is best done early in the placement, so there is a firm base established should future difficulties develop (see Activity 4.1). Students can arrive on placement with varying degrees of preparation for observation. Final-level students will have experienced direct observation already, but first-placement students may be uninformed. It can certainly not be assumed that observation has taken place in students' previous work or educational experience. It is also worth clarifying that it is the student's practice which will be observed and not an assessment of the service users' situation. Although obvious to practice teachers, it is best in early placement stages to assume no knowledge on the student's part.

Activity 4.1 Ground rules

Contents: exercise
Resources: copies of questionnaire
Time needed: one hour

This activity is on setting expectations and ground rules for direct observation. It should be completed by both practice teacher and student and then exchanged. Subsequent discussion can identify common areas, and also differences in expectations, so these can be recognised and resolved before the observation is arranged.

The practice teacher

The practice teacher should complete the following

1. I expect to directly observe the student's practice with service users

1	2	3	4	5

Minimal number   Most of the
of times required   time

2. I expect to observe the student's practice directly

1	2	3	4	5

Early in the   At the end
placement

3. I expect students to participate in direct observation

1	2	3	4	5

Enthusiastically   Reluctantly

4. I regard direct observation to be an assessment method which is

1	2	3	4	5

Very useful   Not useful

5. I regard that as a teaching method direct observation is

1	2	3	4	5

Very useful   Useless

One of the things I like about this method is:

One of the things I dislike about this method is:

When involved in direct observation things I expect a student to consider are:

- -

The student

The student should complete the following:

1. I expect my practice to be observed directly:

| 1 | 2 | 3 | 4 | 5 |

- -

Minimal times
required

Most of the
time

2. I expect to be observed directly:

| 1 | 2 | 3 | 4 | 5 |

- -

Early in the
placement

At the end

3. I expect I will participate in direct observation

| 1 | 2 | 3 | 4 | 5 |

- -

Enthusiastically

Reluctantly

4. I regard direct observation as an assessment method which is:

| 1 | 2 | 3 | 4 | 5 |

- -

Very useful

Useless but
required

5. I consider that as a learning method direct observation is:

| 1 | 2 | 3 | 4 | 5 |

- -

Very useful

Useless

One of the things I like about this method is:

- -

One of the things I dislike about this method is:

- -

When involved in direct observation I expect to consider:

Direct observation of the student's practice presents a situation where assessment is formal and the student is fully aware of this. It is therefore important to clarify with the student early in the placement the approach that a practice teacher intends to adopt towards assessment. This requires a thorough explanation of all assessment methods, and a practice teacher should reserve the right to use them all if necessary. This can prevent future misunderstandings, such as a student complaining that a report contains evidence based one assessment other than formal direct observation, as he was under the impression that these were the only situations when he was being assessed.

At contract stage a practice teacher should emphasise and record her right to use direct observation more than the minimal number of times specified by the programme. This should be re-stated at interim evaluation stage, if a student's progress is regarded as doubtful, and at any other meetings called to 'flag up' possible failure. This should also be recorded and signed by all participants. It is not wise to assume that an anxious or hostile student has absorbed the information that the stated number of required direct observations are only minimal. It avoids a situation where he may complain subsequently that he has been unfairly treated, and his practice observed more than other students or the times specified in the handbook.

Practice teachers' attitudes towards direct observation

When working with a failing student, where direct observation can be a larger part of the process than usual, it is particularly important that a practice teacher examines her own attitudes towards observation, and is reasonably comfortable with the method. It can be particularly important in the few situations where a student's practice is very poor, or malpractice is suspected. In extreme situations, it may in fact be necessary to undertake unannounced direct observation of a student's practice. This runs counter to principles of good practice and the idea that students should be fully involved in the process with consent fully negotiated. Inevitably a practice teacher will feel disappointed if this point is reached, as it is a far cry from the partnership, 'learning together', approach at which placements aim.

Many practice teachers may not themselves have trained in an era when practice was observed. However an increasing number of them are now Practice Teacher Award holders, or training for it, so have had their practice teaching observed by a mentor. This can be an empowering situation for all students, in particular failing students who may be resistant to the assessment process because:

- A practice teacher experiences the same process herself as the student, so has the chance to model a confident approach to it
- A practice teacher is in a better position to assure a student she can understand the stresses of the process if she is undertaking it herself
- The acceptance of direct observation as a customary process for practice teacher as well as students can help create the climate of a learning organisation
- The mentor can act as a sounding board for the practice teacher and subsequently a safeguard for the student. This process can assist in helping a student feel that a second opinion is involved and the practice teacher's competence is monitored. This can increase her credibility with her student so the process seems fairer.

Preparation for direct observation

The successful use of direct observation involves a practice teacher in the use of various practice teaching skills. She needs to:

- Know how to identify the knowledge and skills used in social work and assess them in practice
- Give prompt feedback, sometimes on the spot, about a student's performance
- Maintain a thorough knowledge of the practice curriculum and competences
- Take a back seat and allow a student to learn and struggle to develop skills in a situation in which service users are involved, and where a practice teacher is not in control and might do things differently and more effectively.

If a practice teacher finds this process difficult or lacks confidence in her ability to execute it, she may collude with a student's resistance and need more experience before she can work with a failing student. This is an area of practice teaching where confidence in planning and implementing direct observation is needed. Being aware of observation's advantages and disadvantages can be helpful. (Exercise 4.1 at the end of this chapter provides an opportunity to develop awareness of the advantages and disadvantages of direct observation.)

Direct observation has many advantages in work with failing students:

1. It ensures the student's practice with service users actually happens and is not dependent on the student's recording of it. Reflective evidence is open to interpretation by a student and may merely reflect that he has learned what to say. Direct observation confirms that a student can not only talk about what social work should be but can actually perform it.
2. It provides direct access to a student's practice. It can be difficult for a clever, articulate student to disguise poor practice or inappropriate values for any sustained length of time when being observed, as non-verbal communications are also open to scrutiny.
3. Its implementation can build relationships with students by creating trust and sharing in live practice situations. It also provides the practice teacher with a chance to obtain and evaluate feedback from service users.

However, direct observation also has disadvantages:

1. It is artificial and a student may feel anxious and perform badly to the detriment of service users.
2. It is intrusive for service users who may not always feel empowered to refuse to participate.
3. Students can feel unable to be spontaneous, to take risks and make mistakes which enable learning. This can offset the value of tangible evidence as students may counter that it was not their real practice, as they found the situation too disempowering to allow them to perform competently.

When preparing to observe students' practice, there is a need for clear ground rules and this particularly applies to students who know they are at risk of failure. The anxiety this engenders can make it difficult for them to hear and agree the arrangements. Practice teacher manuals and workshops often assume this method is being used with competent or at least cooperative students, but the realities of practice teaching are sometimes different. Preparation therefore needs to be carefully handled, and it can save time in the long run, if a thorough briefing session is undertaken. In the complex situations which can be involved in direct observation, the practice teacher needs to brief a student carefully on why direct observation is being used:

- Its rationale as an assessment method
- What aspects of practice will be assessed linked to competences and evidence indicators (a student should be involved in this process as much as possible)
- A process for feedback should be established. (Box 4.1.)

Exercise 4.2 at the end of this chapter is role plays providing an opportunity to focus on preparation work with students for direct observation.

Box 4.1   Sample format for feedback on direct observation of practice

Direct observation: Checklist for feedback by practice teacher

1. Student's preparation for session – good/adequate/poor
2. Student's planning for the session
    - Briefing of service users
    - Clarity over the task and purpose
3. Purpose of the session
    - Aim and objectives for the session
4. Introduction – when, where, how
    - Ground rules established, for example, confidentiality
5. Content of the session
    - Achievement of its aims
    - Use of any agenda for the session
    - Flexibility when necessary
6. Process
    - Student's awareness of the dynamics
    - Communication skills
    - Use of language
    - Verbal/non-verbal communication
    - Issues presented by clients – are they recognised and acknowledged by the student?
    - Student's use of power
7. Endings
    - How are they managed by the student
8. Skills demonstrated
    - Development areas
9. Evidence of competence – positive and negative indicators

The student needs to know that direct observation as a formal assessment event is being undertaken. It often has to be set up specifically in a field-work setting, so the student is quite clear on this. In a residential or day care setting, however, it is not always so clear and the specific time and task should be identified. In a direct observation situation, the power imbalance is overt, possibly more than in any other aspect of the placement, so this needs to be addressed. One way of doing this is the identification and agreement of clearly established ground rules.

Activity 4.2   Preparation for direct observation

Contents: exercise
Resources: exercise and handout
Time needed: 30 minutes

This activity helps to focus a practice teacher's thinking around how to prepare students for direct observation and the kind of planning and ground rules needed.

A practice teacher should:

1. Think of a situation where you are planning to observe directly your student's practice.
2. Consider how you should prepare the student for this.
3. Consider your planning and the ground rules and principles that underpin it.
4. Record your reflections and consider them against the handout (Figure 4.).
5. Share your reflections if appropriate with a mentor.

When establishing the ground rules for direct observation a practice teacher needs to:

1. Acknowledge the anxieties the process can create in the student. Recognise the stress that any assessment situation can induce, and that it will be taken into account.
2. Recognise that students and failing ones in particular can feel vulnerable and 'on the spot'. Acknowledging this vulnerability can help create a safe environment, although false reassurance should be avoided.
3. Establish that the student will be involved in evaluating his own performance after the direct observation, and identifying evidence. He will be given reasons for the practice teacher's final judgement.

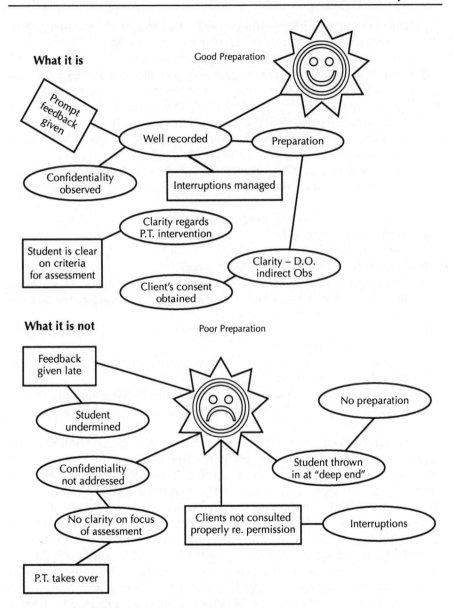

Figure 4.1 Ground rules for direct observation
Adapted from Toussant, et al. (1989)

A practice teacher should plan direct observation in a practice area in which she is experienced herself, otherwise the necessary confidence could be lost in a way which would be disenabling for all involved. This is particularly important in fail situations, if a student subsequently challenges a practice teacher's judgement and appropriate use of power. It may be necessary for her to assert her authority to assess him. This needs to be done from a position of some expertise as a practitioner and teacher. It can be difficult to do if a practice teacher elects to observe a student on practice areas to which she is new herself and feels unsure.

It is advisable to record the agreement for the direct observation. Some suggested points for inclusion are:

- When will the direct observation occur?
- What will be assessed?
- What are the aims of the session?
- How will confidentiality be maintained?
- Selection of service users: decide with the student who will be used, how they will be consulted, the presence of the practice teacher explained and consent obtained
- Be clear on the model used, for example, observation only, or live supervision or joint work
- Identify situations where a practice teacher might intervene, or be consulted by the student
- Agree to give feedback promptly afterwards. If given verbally, record it also.

Several factors need to be taken into account with failing students who might not be cooperating fully with the direct observation process. For example, a student may report that service users are not agreeable to the observation. This may be so, but it is also useful to examine carefully the reasons, and how the student approached it, in case he is wishing to avoid and sabotage efforts to establish the observation. If necessary, a practice teacher needs to be prepared to take over the negotiations for it herself.

Similarly, if a student's practice is particularly weak, a practice teacher may have to intervene, as the protection of service users must be paramount and take precedence over the student's learning and assessment needs. (Exercise 4.4 at the end of this chapter provides a chance to discuss and practice preparation for direct observation and situations where things go wrong.)

Feedback

It is advisable that feedback is always written, to avoid a situation where a student may not hear, or forget it and challenge the practice teacher's final report or the ultimate assessment decision, on the grounds that he was not advised of failure or areas for improvement.

Feedback from others

The involvement of colleagues and other relevant professionals is an invaluable assessment method for students who are failing. It enables a practice teacher to check out her judgement and ensure fairness for students. If all other colleagues involved with a student give positive feedback, then a practice teacher may need to reflect on her own perspective. Similarly a consensus over a student's practice being doubtful would reassure a practice teacher that her judgement is sound and she is not expecting too much. Whatever the circumstances, the involvement of colleagues for use in providing feedback for assessment purposes needs careful structuring:

1. At the pre-placement stage, the team and Line Manager's support for, and involvement in the placement, needs to be negotiated. Team members' involvement in assessment needs clarification, so they can regard the placement as a team one, with the practice teacher managing it, but not left with the sole responsibility.
2. Team members need to be made aware that they may be asked to give feedback which is valued, but the final assessment responsibility rests with the practice teacher.
3. It is essential to plan carefully any direct observations which colleagues provide. It assists if both the colleague and student understand the competences and evidence indicators which the practice observed may cover.

It is important that clarification is made as to how feedback from colleagues will be given to students. A colleague may wish to share some positives immediately after the session, but his/her evidence has to be evaluated by the practice teacher and included in the overall assessment. Negative feedback needs careful handling and may best be delivered in a joint session involving both colleague and student. This means everyone hears what is said. The session should be recorded. This can be particularly important in fail situations, where a student may disagree with the practice teacher's assessment, and try to manipulate the situation to his own advantage, by involving placement colleagues who have praised some aspects of his practice.

Box 4.2   Sample pro forma for direct observation of practice by colleagues

Observer:

Student:

Date and time:

Venue/setting:

Service user(s):

Agreed assessment criteria:

Evaluation of criteria/conclusions:

Signature–Observer   Student:

Date:

When obtaining feedback from others on a student's practice, it is useful to use colleagues who do not always agree with a practice teacher or work the same way. It is also, as regards failing students, advisable to involve other agency workers who do not know that a student is failing. This provides a fresh viewpoint and can help offset any placement collusion which may have developed.

It is usually common knowledge in any placement that a student is failing and colleagues have feelings about this which they may put into the situation, such as denial of the student's poor practice, overprotection of the student and anger towards the practice teacher for upsetting a student whom they may like. A practice teacher may need to try and discuss these feelings and bring them out into the open if she is using her colleagues for feedback. If she is doubtful about her colleagues' judgement, she may need to reassess the situation herself.

Service user involvement in feedback

The use of consumer feedback in student assessment is one of the available methods outlined by CCETSW. Undoubtedly, service users have a perspective which could potentially be of use in estimating the value of a student's practice. Their involvement is essential in situations where students may have falsely claimed to have made contact, and it is necessary to check out the validity of their practice. The concept needs, however, careful application in situations where a student is failing. Possible difficulties may arise around:

- Protection of users' rights not to participate
- Selection of users who would be fair to students, so their selection needs careful consideration
- Protection of users from unfair pressure from students to get a good report. It might shift the focus from users' problems to those of the student.

Indirect observation: video recording of a student's practice

Video recording of a student's practice can be invaluable when working with a student whose competence is doubtful, as it provides 'live' examples of practice available for replay and reflection at a later stage when the participants are not involved. The introduction of the Practice Teacher Award now requires practice teachers to complete a video recording and analysis of their own work with students. This assists with the development of skills in the use of video, both technical and in its use as a teaching and learning method.

The indirect observation provided by video work however needs careful management and it is useful if a practice teacher has thought about the method in advance, particularly regarding its advantages and drawbacks.

Indirect observation has a number of advantages:

1. It is indirect observation which provides a chance to rerun, reflect and check for accuracy, as well as the planning of feedback. It can take a student out of his practice situation and can sometimes assist with his recognising areas for development.
2. It is appropriate for the assessment of interpersonal skills, such as handling of an interview, listening skills or lack of them. Non-verbal communication is also recorded, so oppressive body language is captured, as is lack of assertion. Poor practice is less easily and consistently disguised by a student on video.
3. A video recording also provides tangible, concrete evidence for others to judge. This is fair to a student, particularly if he disagrees the practice teacher's assessment. It also removes any disagreement about what was actually said or happened and it allows a record independent of filters imposed in live observation.
4. The chance to share the evidence with other practice teachers or a mentor can be invaluable if the practice teacher has doubts about her judgement, or there is a personality clash with the student, or the practice teacher's opinion is not shared by colleagues.
5. It records the student's practice in a situation where a practice teacher has concern, but a tutor or line manager may be supportive to the student, and question the validity of the placement and the practice teacher's skills.

However, there are disadvantages to using indirect observation:

1. The technical and time-consuming problems of finding equipment and suitable situations and venues should never be underestimated.
2. It can be stressful for students, as well as artificial. Students may feel they are acting or 'performing' and consequently being tested on skills which are not part of the assessment. They can also challenge it as a valid assessment method, if they find the method so inimical that they cannot show their real practice and are actually performing worse than when not on video.

The use of video requires careful preparation and its success will to some extent depend on the approach of the university and whether it is regularly included in the student's training in the context of a secure learning environment. The practice teacher needs to cover various aspects of preparation with students, including:

- Clarity as to the purpose of the video and the competences to be assessed
- Outline of the advantages of the video work for both student and practice teacher if the student is reluctant to use it
- A supportive approach towards the student's anxieties is needed, but it is also useful to recognise the need to be able to control some of those anxieties in professional qualification training
- Confidentiality – outline how this should be safeguarded and advise on any agency policies on the use of service users in video regarding consent, exclusions and the treatment of tapes afterwards.

As in all assessment methods where students are practising with service users, a yardstick for their use is the student's safety to practice and this applies certainly to the use of video, as the practice teacher is not there to intervene if necessary. If a practice teacher believes that she cannot allow a student to work independently with users then this situation could constitute eventual failure. However video could be used in meetings with colleagues, or in role play, as these situations can sometimes assist the student in developing the necessary skills, and if not, provide the necessary evidence of incompetence.

Some students are totally resistant to the use of video, or even occasionally phobic. In such situations it seems unrealistic to insist on its use. However if a practice teacher considers it would constitute invaluable evidence, obtainable in no other way, she should refer to this in her assessment report, and state the reason the student gave which prevented its use. Failing situations are potentially litigious, so if a practice teacher is unable to use an assessment method she considered particularly valid, this needs noting. It also prevents a student subsequently appealing that assessment was not properly carried out, as video would have demonstrated competence.

On a more positive note, many students welcome video work, recognising its validity and the chance for them to provide additional evidence of their competence, if they consider their practice teacher to be unfair or lacking in the necessary skills.

The assessment of failing students requires a practice teacher to be as sure of her decision as possible. Sound assessment skills are needed, involving the ability to identify social work skills, to model, teach and enable their development and to give feedback on them as well as manage the failing process.

This can only be achieved if a practice teacher is confident in her decision. It is one which in the last resort is subjective, based on expertise and professional judgement but also involving decisions about minimal standards in social work practice and what is 'good enough'.

Exercise 4.1   *Direct observation: advantages and disadvantages*

Contents: discussion exercise and role play
Resources: facilitators, flipchart paper
Time needed: one and a half hours

The aims of this exercise are to:

- Raise awareness of the advantages and disadvantages of direct observation
- Develop skills in overcoming student resistance to direct observation.

Ideally this exercise should be done with a group of practice teachers who are used to working with each other. The group size should be 10–12. The practice teachers should work in pairs and share any anxieties about undertaking direct observation of students. They do not have to share these with the whole group. The group should then divide into two groups.

- Group A: Discuss the advantages of direct observation as a practice teaching method
- Group B: Discuss the disadvantages of direct observation as a practice teaching method.

Both groups should feedback on flipchart paper which can be pinned around the room with time provided for consideration of the ideas.

The next part of the exercise is to give practice teachers an opportunity to practice dealing with the anxieties of students who are worried or resistant to being observed directly in their practice. Participants should divide into groups of three. The previous groups A and B should be mixed. In each small group, one practice teacher should take the role of student, one the role of practice teacher, and one should act as observer.

They should role play a scenario where a student on a first placement is asking why she must be observed. She should use the disadvantages discussed as a reason for questioning the validity of it as a practice teaching method. The practice teacher should attempt to counter and overcome her reluctance. Time should be allowed after the role plays for discussion and the observer to feedback on the validity of the arguments and their effectiveness.

This exercise can be adapted for mentor support workshops, to prepare them to work with practice teachers who are anxious at having their practice with students observed.

Exercise 4.2   Preparation for direct observation

Contents: role play exercise
Resources: facilitators, cards with scenario and briefings, video cameras
Time needed: one and a half hours

This exercise aims to:

- Enable practice teachers to develop skills in preparing for direct observation with resistant students
- Practice supervising students on video
- Develop skills in giving feedback on both direct and indirect observation
- Experience being observed in a situation similar to students.

This exercise, based on role play is best undertaken with a small group of practice teachers and recorded on video in the process. Ideally, it is done with a group who meet regularly and feel safe to share practice. The exercise requires one participant to act as the student and the rest of the group to take the role of practice teacher in turn. The participant who is the student takes this role throughout the exercise, and plays it with each practice teacher in the group.

The facilitator stops the video at appropriate intervals, plays it back and the group discusses the practice teacher's performance. The role play and video then continue from the point where it was stopped, with a new practice teacher taking the session further until all participants have played practice teacher. Each practice teacher should try to deal with the student's resistance to role play and to bring out his real underlying anxieties. At the end of the role play the group discusses both the situation and the ways it was handled.

Scenario for the role play (shared with the whole group)

A practice teacher and student are discussing the student's preparation for direct observation of practice. It is halfway into the placement and interim evaluation is due. No direct observation has yet been done. The student clearly dislikes the idea, but insists he has tried to arrange it with the selected service users who have refused to agree to it. The practice teacher arranged one direct observation but the student was ill and absent from the placement. By this stage the practice teacher suspects that the student is sabotaging efforts to organise direct observation and the service users' refusal may reflect that. She is wondering if the student is ashamed of his practice and trying to avoid scrutiny. The role play is an enactment of the discussion where the practice teacher confronts the student with the lack of progress, and expresses concern that at this late stage of the placement he faces failure if the situation cannot be resolved.

She tries to deal with any anxieties the student may have about the observation as well as the reason for the delay. The student responds aggressively. He denies any difficulty and launches into an attack on direct observation as an assessment method. He considers it is an intrusion on service users and damaging to the relationship he has established with them.

Briefing for the student (shared with the whole group)

A male experienced residential worker, on a first placement in an area office. He has difficulty understanding professional boundaries. He becomes over-involved with service users and promises confidences will remain secret and confidential to him alone. He discloses his own difficulties about his marital problems to a family he is working with, so they will know he understands what it is like to have problems and to come from a broken home. He is in fact gaining a fair bit of emotional support from his service users and is beginning to focus on his problems not theirs. He has been on the course long enough to realise that his practice may be questioned, and does not want his practice teacher to see him in operation. In the role play therefore he insists the service users will not cooperate and attacks direct observation as a valid method. The arguments he uses against direct observation are that:

- Direct observation is a breach of confidence
- The service users will not trust him afterwards
- The service users will lose confidence if his practice teacher has to check upon him
- He cannot show his real practice if observed
- He will be too anxious to practice properly.

Exercise 4.3   *Further preparation for direct observation*

Content: role plays
Resources: facilitators, role play briefings
Time needed: one hour

This exercise is divided into two stages and aims to:

- Focus practice teachers on the process of preparation for direct observation
- Develop skills in preparing students to prepare for direct observation.

Stage one

This exercise should be done with small groups of practice teachers working in groups of threes. One participant should take the role of practice teacher, one the role of student, and one the role of observer. Each triad can work on different role plays. Time should then be allowed for general discussion of the issues raised and the observer can feedback on how the situations were addressed.

A)   Enact a student and practice teacher discussing how the student will ask for service users' consent to direct observation of an interview with them. The student responds positively to the idea, but unsure how to go about it and how to explain the practice teacher's presence.

B)   Enact a situation where a student has attempted to gain the service users' consent but has come back and said that they refused and did not want a student working with them.

C)   Enact a situation where a student is resistant to the whole idea of direct observation. He accepts it must happen but is most unhappy that it is artificial, stressful and does not suit his learning style. He thinks it makes use of service users for his benefit and training needs.

Stage two

Content: discussion exercise
Resources: facilitators, prepared discussion cards
Time needed: one hour

This stage can be done independently, with a mentor or a colleague or in a group. The practice teachers should independently or in pairs discuss several or all of the situations listed below, all of which pertain to situations of direct observation:

- Your student is excessively nervous and 'dries up'
- Your student seeks advice from you in the interview on a legal matter and then disagrees the accuracy of your information

- Your student makes blatant sexist or racist or other oppressive remarks
- Your student gets into a mess – bursts into tears or runs out of the room
- Your student gives incorrect information on an important Agency policy
- The service user becomes verbally aggressive and the student cannot handle it to the point where you are concerned his safety may be at risk
- The student self discloses inappropriately and begins to present his problems for the service user to deal with
- The student sticks rigidly to the agenda and plan for the interview made on the referral point and ignores an important disclosure from the service user regarding for example, a child protection issue; suicidal feelings.

Reflection/discussion pointers

- How would you handle this?
- Has a similar situation happened to you? How did you handle it?
- Consider the current ground rules you establish with students on direct observation
- Consider whether you need to change your current ground rules in future work with students or whether your existing ones cover the potential for situations to go wrong.

If this exercise is done in a group, time should be allowed for sharing of ideas by the whole group and discussion around the preparation and ground rules needed for direct observation of students' practice when all does not go smoothly.

Exercise 4.4   *Practising assessment in direct observation*

Content: discussion exercise
Resources: a scenario, modelled live or a prepared video
Time Needed: one hour

The aims of the exercise are to:

- Assist practice teachers to overcome anxieties about undertaking direct observation
- Develop skills in undertaking direct observation

- Raise awareness of the range of perspectives which can emerge in assessment.

This exercise needs to be done with a group of practice teachers. The group facilitators, possibly using a volunteer(s) from the group, should model a scenario, identified in advance, where a student is working with service user(s). Alternatively a prepared video recording can be used.

One possible scenario

A final placement student is undertaking an interview with an elderly woman who has been referred by her GP as in need of residential care. Initial discussion indicates she wishes to remain in her own home. She is prepared to consider services at home. Her daughter lives nearby and works full-time. She is concerned about her mother and is pressurising the doctor to get some assistance for her. She has taken time off and is at the interview with her mother's agreement, although they did not tell the student about this in advance. Model the student's handling of this situation.

The practice teacher group should observe the enactment of this scenario and attempt to identify the knowledge and skills the student is demonstrating. They should then complete a checklist prepared by the facilitators in advance which is linked to the assessment report of the DipSW programme with which the group works. They should then work in small groups of three and share ideas on the competence level of the student and how they found doing the exercise. The larger group can then, if time allows, spend some time discussing the observation process: what created anxiety about it? What was reassuring about it?

5 Good enough practice

Determining minimal levels of satisfactory practice

Defining the minimal level of competent practice acceptable at qualification point is perhaps one of the most difficult tasks facing a practice teacher. It is also one of the most important, as it decides who obtains a social worker qualification, which awards the right to work with service users and can become a gateway to a range of jobs, and an extensive career structure within caring organisations.

Making the decision about 'good enough' practice is not always easy for inexperienced practice teachers. It is often made easier by work with a range of students, as this provides the necessary opportunity for comparison. It is usually only after they have done this that practice teachers can feel at ease working with borderline students and making Fail decisions.

This experience is needed because of the imprecise nature of assessment around marginal standards. It provides practice teachers with a basis for reflecting on their previous decisions. It is not at all unusual to hear practice teachers comment that the decision over which they agonised regarding students early in their practice teaching career became much clearer once it could be put in the context of other students' practice. Once they meet a student whose practice they feel sure is insufficient, then they have a valuable yardstick. This reinforces the value of the current developing trend in practice teaching for aspiring practice teachers to operate first as workplace supervisors under the auspices of accredited practice teachers, acting in a 'long arm' capacity. This can hopefully prevent the situation where practice teachers only gain the experience necessary for determining minimal standards by first passing students whose practice is dubious.

It is also to be hoped that the opportunity for practice teachers to gain experience and consolidate skills by practice teaching regularly, which is now a requirement for accreditation, will assist with this task of assessing minimal standards.

The difficulties and dilemmas involved

When observing students' practice, it is often quite easy to recognise whether their performance is good or poor, but less easy to say why and at what standard it should be executed. The task of deciding whether a student is ready to qualify requires an understanding of what good social work practice is, and the minimum level students need to attain. A minority of students may practice superbly, and a similar small number do so quite horrendously. In such situations the assessment decision is clear, even if its implementation is painful. Students whose practice is 'borderline' can present the dilemmas and sleepless nights, as these require making complex decisions around what is 'good enough' practice. This can pose real dilemmas for a group of practice teachers, themselves trained in a low failure culture, who consequently, in their own professional backgrounds, have few models to draw upon regarding minimum levels, when it is necessary to fail students, and how to do it.

Many practice teachers will know fellow students from their own training days or colleagues whom they consider should not have qualified. However, once faced themselves with deciding whether to fail a borderline student, the difficulties become apparent:

- There is a lack of clear, nationally determined criteria for minimal practice, with few processes for achieving standardisation
- There exist no nationally determined professional standards policy, with a code of practice for students across the programme, in both university and placement, and linked explicitly to termination of training procedures. Efforts to develop these are dependent on local initiatives amongst DipSW programmes
- Many practice teachers work as 'singletons' and lack therefore a chance to work with a group of students, which would enable them to compare and develop ideas about acceptable borderline standards and the appropriateness of their expectations
- Some practice teachers work in isolated settings. They can be the only social worker attached to a multidisciplinary team or voluntary or-

ganisation, and they lack feedback from other social work colleagues to allow them to check out their own perception

- Practice teachers may work in settings where there are few qualified social workers, or where several years post-qualifying experience is required before appointment. This can mean they become out of touch with newly qualified workers, the level of skills newcomers possess when coming to a team and the expectation it is realistic to have of them.

When assessing minimal standards the process can feel very subjective. The competence assessment framework outlined by CCETSW attempts to reduce 'assessment by intuition' to which Kadushin (1976) refers, by outlining indicators for the evidence to be used. Linking judgement to competencies and evidence only reduces the element of subjectivity in assessment. Within a competence there is always scope for skills development and the need therefore to decide whether this has occurred at a level sufficient for a student to practice at qualification point. It is in the grey area of minimal standards that a practice teacher feels very aware that, in the last resort, it is her professional judgement which is the deciding factor as to whether the evidence from a student's practice is sufficient.

The particular DipSW programme with which a practice teacher is working can sometimes aggravate the difficulties. The assessment framework provided can be in the form of a complex and off-putting checklist, which appears to invite practice teachers to focus on providing evidence that a student is ready to practice, without any integration of negative indicators or space for reasons why practice is inadequate. It is essential therefore that a practice teacher checks each programme's handbook regarding requirement and guidelines regarding standards of practice, as variations occur:

- Some programmes may include helpful negative as well as positive indicators
- Some set a different, lower standard for first level than for second
- Some place a formal expectation on students to identify their own learning needs and to integrate them into the curriculum, with an expectation on students to provide evidence of competence for inclusion in the assessment report.

The process of identifying 'good enough' practice

CCETSW's (1991, revised 1995) guidelines do not define minimal standards for determining adequate practice. Within the six core competencies, each has a practice requirement and evidence indicator. Each indicator identifies the activities a student may be expected to undertake to provide the evidence that they have met the practice requirements for competence. However: 'Programme providers ... particularly practice teachers *must* judge the quality, coherence and sufficiency of the evidence provided by students to show that they have met the practice requirements.'

This is no easy task and is one in which a practice teacher clearly has a key role. It is up to individual Programmes to assist with identifying detailed criteria for deciding whether a student is competent. It can in fact be left to practice teachers to do this.

The assessment that a student's practice is insufficient requires the ability to identify social work knowledge and skills, recognise them in practice and know when they are being satisfactorily performed. A practice teacher also has to be clear when she is not finding what she is looking for, and give reasons as to why practice is at an insufficient level of competence. This is easier if she knows and can record the criteria for both good and bad practice when assessing her student. There are several ways in which these can be identified:

- Some programmes provide guidelines on negative as well as positive indicators
- Practice teacher workshops can provide an opportunity for practice teachers to check out with others what they are looking for and how realistic their standards and expectations are.

Workshops can also provide invaluable opportunities to discuss case scenarios which assist with the resolution of difficulties. (Exercise 5.1 at the end of this chapter outline examples of these.)

If a practice teacher cannot access a support group, then she could work with a mentor to define minimal standards and determine whether a student's practice meets them. Alternatively a practice teacher colleague could assist, particularly one who has some experience of failing students. This provides an informal second opinion. It is important to protect confidentiality and ideally the student should know of this contact. Video work of a student's practice can be useful, but it is not always easy to obtain this and certainly a student's consent should be obtained if sharing a video of his practice with a colleague.

Box 5.1   Checklist: Positive and negative indicators of competence
(adapted from Brandon and Davies 1979)

Core competence: communicate and engage
Suggested evidence indicators

a)   Establish initial contact and the reason for it with service users:

Positive indicators	*Negative indicators*
Negotiates contact	Imposes intervention
Collects necessary information in advance	Imposes intervention
Plans initial contact	Arrives unannounced without good reason
Clarifies the purpose of contact	Purpose is unclear
Explains agency role, powers for intervention	Does not clarify agency role, set goals or explain rationale for intervention
Forms a contract	Contract is unclear
Involves users in contract	Contract ignores users

b)   Communicate effectively and develop working relationships with service users:

Positive indicators	*Negative indicators*
Listens, attends and responds sensitively	Cannot focus
Summarises and allows for reflection	Hesitant interviewer
Recognises and accepts differences	Intolerant of differences
Recognises power in own role	Indifferent to power
Structures interviews and responds to users pace	Cannot lead interview
Understands boundaries	Collusive or over-friendly
Engages own emotions appropriately	Cannot deal with own feelings

These suggested indicators are by no means definitive but outline an approach to developing indicators, which can provide a scale for identifying a student's position.

Box 5.2   Guidelines for identifying appropriate levels of student competence by the end of each placement, linked to the values which CCETSW requires for each practice requirement

Awareness of power/oppression
The scale below provides ideas as to where a student should be at various stages of the placement process:

Unskilled practice	*End of first placement*	*End of second placement*
Unaware of issues power/oppression experienced by disadvantaged groups	Can acknowledge the power which a social worker possesses. Can identify oppressive behaviour	Positively identifies issues. Able to confront and challenge oppressive behaviour

This example can be used to develop ideas around expectations about the level appropriate to each placement across the competencies.

If a practice teacher works in an isolated setting and cannot access workshops, or is too busy to get to them, then a simplistic, but often helpful checklist can sometimes focus a gut feeling of unease:

- Is your student ready to move on to a second placement? Would you want him in your placement?
- Would there be time in a second placement to address the students learning needs? Is he taking an excessively long list of major development needs to another placement or his first social work job?
- Would you really prefer this student to repeat a first placement, to consolidate learning before progressing on to a final placement?
- Does this student, given more time, have the potential to become a social worker?
- Would you want this student as a newly qualified worker in your setting? If not, why would anyone else? Where should he go?
- Do you really want to fail this student but do not feel strong enough to do it?
- Are you happy to stake your professional reputation on signing that this student is ready to pass this placement/practice as a qualified social worker?
- Would you feel happy with this student working with one of your relatives in a professional capacity?

Activity 5.1   Identifying minimal levels of practice

Contents: discussion exercise
Resources: scale and case study
Time needed: one hour

This activity encourages reflection around the appropriate level of practice for a student at the end of the first and second placement. It provides a basis for practice teachers to form their own ideas about standards and identify with colleagues the basis for common ground. This activity can be done independently, or with a group of practice teachers working in pairs, or by two colleagues or a practice teacher and a mentor. It assists with the identification of levels of practice sufficient to demonstrate competence and the reasons for this.

A practice teacher should consider the following scale in respect to the need to challenge oppression and a student's attitude and skills in doing so:

A	B	C
Compliance	Identification	Internalisation
Student can recognise oppression. Regards challenging it as necessary to obtain the DipSW.	Challenging oppression represents the values of the student/placement team and practice teacher which he shares. He can demonstrate the competence within the group. He may lose the commitment and ability without its reinforcement	The need to challenge oppression is part of the student as a person and professional

The practice teacher should estimate at what point a student needs to be as regards the ability to challenge oppressive practice, in order to obtain a:

Pass at a final placement. Circle the point on the scale:

Pass at first placement	A	A/B	B	B/C	C
Pass at final placement	A	A/B	B	B/C	C

The practice teacher should then consider examples of their own student's practice and consider at what level the student is at.

The following scenario can also be considered:

Whilst on placement the student heard a colleague make a highly racist joke and he laughed at it. His practice teacher challenged him. The student said his response was spontaneous and he regretted it afterwards, as he knows from the teaching on the DipSW course that social workers should condemn such behaviour. He expressed surprise that a social work colleague had made the joke and no one had told him off.

Reflection pointers:

- Where does this response put this student on the scale?
- Assuming there is no change during the placement should this student pass?
- Would the practice described be sufficient for a student to pass a first placement but not a second?

This scale can be adapted to cover other practice requirements.

Although unrefined, this kind of reflection can give some yardstick for clarifying decisions when a student's practice is borderline. They also help to focus on the cause for concern.

The need for self-awareness

When dealing with issues around borderline students, a practice teacher needs to be aware of her own personal agenda on failure, so she can be alert to this influencing her assessment. For example, a practice teacher who experienced a poor practice placement herself, or finds the idea of failure intolerable, may feel she has to compensate for this with her own students and that failing will be letting them down. Similarly a practice teacher may feel her job is to 'help' a student through, so she blocks on recognising a student's deficiencies, in case this reflects on the adequacy of the placement she offers.

As a background to all assessment but particularly in the area of minimal standards, she needs to reflect on her own experiences of and response to failure. This helps foster self-awareness on whether failure is something she will always want to avoid, whether her expectations are likely to be too lenient or stringent, and whether she is likely to be too hard on herself as a practice teacher. In an assessment situation no one can get it right all the time. An acceptance of this can lead to a more relaxed attitude and increased capacity to work in the area of minimal standards.

Activity 5.2   Thinking around failure

Content: exercise
Resources: copies of questionnaire
Time needed: 45 minutes

This activity promotes awareness on personal attitudes to failure and issues around its assessment. This activity can be completed with a mentor, or by a group of practice teachers working in pairs. Issues, but not the personal content, should be shared in discussion afterwards, to look at how attitudes/experience of failure can affect an approach to the assessment task and assessment skills.

Questions for discussion

- Did you fail or nearly fail either of your own placements when you were a student? If yes: How was it handled? How did it affect you?
  If no: How would you have felt about failing your placement(s)?
- How stringent was the assessment you experienced as a student?
- How was giving negative feedback handled?
- How would you have liked it to be handled?
- If failing a student yourself how does your own experience as a student inform your practice teaching?

- How do you regard situations where you fail?

1	2	3	4	5
Very seriously				Unconcerned

- What are your standards for yourself?

1	2	3	4	5
Perfectionist	Stringent	Reasonable	Easy-going	Sloppy

- What are your standards for others?

1	2	3	4	5
Very high	High	Reasonable	Easy-going	Too lenient

- Do you think if a student works hard enough success will be achieved?
- Do you think all students selected by a programme ought to able to pass their placements.?
- What is your response to a student who shows academic laziness? Poor motivation? Only enough effort to get through the placement?

Involving students in determining minimal standards

When assessing students and deciding what is adequate practice, it is a valuable exercise to involve students in identifying the standard required. It is particularly important with borderline students to try and help them understand what is required:

- A sample appointment letter or report written to the required standard could be shown as a guide
- A sample work plan so the student can gain some idea of acceptable practice within the placement
- Some examples of what a practice teacher will be looking for when a student engages with people. This can be done by role play or a video of an intervention.

Ideally this should include clarification on which competence is being assessed and the criteria identifying what a practice teacher wants, and does not want to see in a student's practice. Involving a student in defining what are indicators of poor practice can sometimes be just what he needs to enable him to recognise blocks in his learning and move on. It helps create a safe learning and assessment situation. However the process may not always be as easy as the manuals on good practice teaching imply, as a few students may resist assessment, particularly if alerted to the possibility of failing a placement.

A practice teacher can then find that a student disagrees with what she is looking for. She may have to be prepared to assert the right to assess certain tasks and criteria in the event of a student wishing to avoid assessment of weak areas or not recognising the skills needed. For example, a student who has difficulty engaging with people might want to focus on the ability to meet deadlines, resolve practical issues and stress the need for detachment, boundaries and control of emotions.

It is therefore possible for the situation to occur where the practice teacher and student disagree on what constitutes good social work practice, and the criteria for assessing its effective performance. If serious conflict exists it is best brought out from the start, so ways can be sought for its resolution. In the last resort if this cannot be achieved, then the supervisory relationship may break down and the placement terminate, but it is often better for this to happen at an earlier rather than later stage.

This kind of situation requires confidence in a practice teacher and the ability, if necessary, to insist on the right to assess, and to determine why certain criteria are being used and the appropriate standard.

Student's problems which affect their performance

Other factors can cause difficulties when working with students whose practice is borderline. The task of deciding whether a student's practice is good enough for him to pass the placement can be confused by difficulties pertaining to a student's personal circumstances. A student may face failure for reasons which are beyond his control. A practice teacher can subsequently find herself assessing a student's abilities to practice competently and handle the stress of social work, in a situation where a student struggles with difficulties which would not exist if he were a salaried member of staff.

Student poverty can be a factor influencing progress. It reflects current funding policies, and a retraction in agency sponsorship and secondments. The resultant financial difficulties produced may not always be expected initially by a practice teacher, as many have undertaken their own professional training in a different economic climate. The extent to which these can be taken into account as mitigating factors when determining minimal levels of competent practice can subsequently cause a lot of heart searching.

The kinds of practical difficulties a student can encounter which impact on placements are many and may require placement extensions. These kinds of situations are expanded on in Chapter 8. They necessitate the need for flexibility in assessment situations, but a practice teacher still has to ensure sufficient practice is completed and the assessment requirements are met.

A practice teacher needs to distinguish between a student's basic ability to practice competently, or whether his performance is poor because of pressures specific to the student situation. This means deciding whether a student lacks the necessary skills or could meet the practice requirements at a sufficiently competent level, if his financial or practical problems were eliminated. For example, in situations of irregular attendance on placement or unreliability, a practice teacher must assess whether a student has a fundamental difficulty in coping with conflicting time demands and personal/work pressure, or whether the difficulty genuinely reflects the student's circumstances and would be resolved if he could fund adequate child care, or run a reliable car.

If a practice teacher considers a student's practice could be competent but the assessment is blurred by extraneous and mitigating circumstances, it may be necessary to consider the potential for a part-time placement, to relieve the pressure on the student. This needs discussion with the university and agency as to whether it can be managed and resourced.

This is not an easy situation and a practice teacher has to balance diverse and conflicting pressures and make tough decisions. In the last resort a student has to demonstrate competence. If a potentially competent student is vulnerable and struggling to succeed, then initially the benefit of the doubt in assessment may be given. However a cut-off point must come. Service users are also vulnerable and must not bear the burden of the doubt. If external pressures on a student cannot be resolved, so he can perform competently, then failure is inevitable. Under DipSW assessment, mitigating circumstances cannot prevail against the need for students to practice competently.

The level of support which is viable

When deciding on what is 'good enough' a practice teacher needs to decide how much input and support from her is justifiable. Often students whose practice is weak make the necessary progress, if given additional support and supervision time. It is tempting to provide unlimited support as a practice teacher often likes her student and wants him to succeed. However this can cause dilemmas, as a student needs to demonstrate competent practice by the end of the placement, and to do this with some ability to work independently, and control his own learning and future development professionally.

A practice teacher can therefore feel uneasy if the student seems to be getting through the placement by excessive dependence on her and her colleagues. This creates concern as to whether he will function in a real work situation. Similar difficulties can occur with academic work which the student needs to complete whilst on placement, such as practice studies. A DipSW programme will usually clarify expectations regarding the practice teacher's on this. However it is not unknown for a student to seek considerable assistance with this work and practice teachers may be concerned that it is becoming more theirs than the student's.

These dilemmas are often resolvable once recognised and addressed. Many borderline students can benefit from extra support but it needs careful structuring:

- Most programmes lay down recommended expectations for supervision, often weekly. In final placements it is sometimes formally agreed that this will reduce towards the end of the placement, so the student prepares for the expectations regarding frequency of supervision for qualified staff. Even if this does not happen, a practice teacher can still satisfy herself that the student can use supervision from a position of being able to work independently
- If the student needs considerably more help than is within the agreed contract, and this seems to be on a regular rather than an occasional basis, then it is often best to formalise this at a special meeting with the tutor or at an interim evaluation stage. Particular circumstances can sometimes justify extra support. Occasionally a student arrives on a final placement and it is clear that the first placement, through no fault of the student's, was unsatisfactory and did not provide the necessary opportunity for him to attain the required level for a final placement to build upon
- If it seems that a student has the necessary potential to demonstrate the required competence with additional support then this can often be agreed, although an extended placement may be needed. This is often the best way forward, as it provides time both for the student to receive the extra input, and also for it to be reduced, so the necessary competent practice can be shown working within the usual support structure
- Dilemmas over minimal standards, and the appropriate level of support, can often be clarified by considering the kind of expectations placed on newly qualified social workers in a work setting. The amount of support offered them, as well as the level of competence expected, can be a guide with a final placement student soon to qualify.

(Exercise 5.2 at the end of this chapter provides an opportunity to practice identifying minimal standards.)

Is it me?

When working with borderline students, a common dilemma for a practice teacher is whether her skills are good enough, particularly when meeting her first situation where failure is possible. This anxiety needs to be addressed, otherwise a practice teacher may collude with poor student practice as a result of concerns about her own. The practice teacher – student working relationship is a close one – they often are in the same team and share the same room. It is therefore not unusual for a practice teacher when determining minimal standards for her student to feel the situation has become so close that she is assessing her own practice.

Similarly a practice teacher can wonder if her standards are too high and she is expecting too much. This difficulty is compounded by the reality that in social work education there exists models of experienced and unqualified social workers gaining admission to DipSW courses. This can raise the profile of students in both age range, life experience and social work experience. The social work profession does not necessarily expect qualification before employment, and this can lead to a practice teacher basing her assessment on minimal standards at too high a starting point. A minimal requirement of six months is placed on social work entrants for pre-course experience in an activity related to social work. A practice teacher needs to take this into account when assessing minimal standards, so she can achieve realistic expectations on what students can do at the start of their training. The job is around training students new to professional activity, who are 'green', as is the common parlance.

There are no clear answers to these dilemmas. The following checklist sometimes assists, as it enables a practice teacher to weigh up whether the placement has provided the opportunity for the student to make the necessary learning.

Dealing with the marginal issues involved in the assessment of social work can promote a practice teacher's confidence in working with failing students. This is particularly necessary when approaching the task of telling the student that he is failing and writing the assessment report.

Box 5.3   Checklist: Has the placement been adequate?

- Practice learning agreement: have all the agreed opportunities been provided?
- Contract: was thorough contract work undertaken? Has it been maintained/reviewed?
- Work selected: has it allowed the student the chance to provide the necessary practice opportunity to demonstrate competence? If not, have other opportunities been sought?
- Was the team prepared for the student and have they provided appropriate support?
- Has supervision been provided and records kept? If cancelled, by whom?
- Have a variety of assessment methods been used, linked to the student's learning style?
- Has the assessment been based on the identified competence? Was the student aware of what was expected?
- If the practice teacher was away sick, did the student receive adequate support and supervision during this period?
- Have the meetings with the student's tutor been undertaken?
- Has feedback from others been obtained so the assessment is varied?
- Has consultancy, or second opinion been sought if there is concern about the student's practice?
- Has information been provided about the university-taught input, for example, expectations about legal knowledge need to be underpinned by an awareness of what the student has been taught, so an appropriate expectation can be identified?

Exercise 5.1   Assessing good enough practice

Stage 1

Content: assessment exercise
Resources: facilitators; model or video a student's practice, flipchart, competence example
Time needed: one and a half hours

This exercise is designed to:

- Develop skills in assessing minimal levels of practice
- Develop skills in evidencing incompetent practice.

This exercise is designed to be done with a group of practice teachers and requires two facilitators. A volunteer from the participants can also be recruited. The facilitators should enact a scenario of a student's practice. It can also include the presence of a practice teacher who is directly observing the student's practice. The scenario should show the student interacting with a service user and failing to engage. The interaction should be modelled for 20–25 minutes. The student's practice should not be so incompetent that the observer has to intervene. It could be recorded on video so it can be replayed later to allow for more detailed reflection and discussion. Alternatively the modelling can be videoed in advance and played back for the discussion.

The practice teachers should work independently and prepare feedback for the student on his practice, to identify the effectiveness or ineffectiveness of his knowledge, skills, and values. Practice teachers should then work in pairs; share their feedback and link it to the Core skills and assessment proforma from a DipSW programme, which the facilitators should provide.

Stage 2

Content: assessment exercise
Resources: facilitators, case study examples
Time needed: one hour

This exercise is designed to:

- Develop practice teacher skills in assessing minimal standards of practice
- Develop practice teacher skills in identifying a framework for evidencing these decisions.

This exercise should be done with a group of practice teachers, working in threes. They should discuss the following scenario and their expectations of a first-level student, by the end of the placement on recognising and challenging oppression. The focus should be the assessment of the student's observations skills, values and ability to identify oppressive practices. The group should then prepare feedback for the student. They should reach a majority decision as to whether it is sufficiently competent, with reasons. The small groups should then discuss their feedback with the whole group.

Scenario

A student is in the last four weeks of her first placement. She has already shown some difficulty in recognising oppression, although when she does she can challenge it quite confidently. For example, she tackled a colleague who made a blatantly racist joke in the office. She has a background as a home carer and thinks women now have more opportunity than ever. She is delighted to have her opportunity to train as a social worker.

She thinks any young woman who gets pregnant without the means to support a child in modern-day society, with the family planning available, is irresponsible, and should not expect state benefit. She has been advised by her practice teacher that there are concerns about her punitive remarks to single parents. She showed herself capable of caring, empathic work, grounded in sound common sense with a young woman whose husband died. She has been asked to keep a daily log and record any instances of oppressive practice she encounters. She attended a case conference as an observer. It was to review the situation of a child on the child protection register who had been left alone. The panel was predominantly male. The mother and child were present, but the child was crying and this disturbed the meeting. The chair asked for a social work assistant to be called to care for the child whilst the conference continued. A female SWA arrived and took the child away; his cries were heard throughout the building until the meeting concluded its business. The mother had been distracted for the rest of the meeting. The student recorded the details clearly and concisely. She regarded it as a regrettable event and noted the effect on the child and the 'messages' being given the mother. She was however sympathetic to the manager's need to get the job done. She did not question managerial and institutional practices. Her comments were that the mother should have made other arrangements for the child and not brought him to the case conference.

Exercise 5.2   Is our practice good enough?

Content: discussion exercise
Resources: facilitators, list of indicators, a scenario to model or prepared video, flipchart
Time needed: one to one and a half hours

The aims of this exercise are to:

- Focus on identifying indicators of poor practice
- Develop skills in assessment.

This exercise should be done by a group of practice teachers who ideally are used to working together and sharing practice. It gives them a chance to exchange ideas on what constitutes poor social work practice, as well as to develop confidence in their own judgement and recognise the range of perspectives involved in assessment.

The group should initially work in pairs and be given an example of a competence and a list of negative indicators. One example is given below. The group should discuss this for 5–10 minutes, to see if they agree the list or to make additions. Then working in the same pairs, they should be given another competence and asked to identify their own list of negative indicators. They should list these on to a flipchart and share this with the whole group.

The facilitators can then model a student with a service user(s), or a prepared video can be watched. The group should assess the role play and, working individually, should prepare a checklist of indicators of poor practice. This should be fed back to the whole group.

Communicate and engage

Practice requirement: Network and form effective working relationships with and between individual agencies, community resources and other professionals.

Evidence indicator: Establish contact with individuals, agencies, community resources, volunteers and other professionals.

Negative indicators

The student:

- patronises volunteer workers
- upsets other agency professionals unjustifiably
- poor letter/report writing
- fails to observe confidentiality
- tactless
- lacks confidence in approach to other agencies
- fails to understand the role of other agencies
- puts members of the medical profession on a pedestal and defers to them
- fails to communicate/advocate.

6 Telling the student and recording the decision

Failure seems likely

Telling a student he is failing his placement is one of the more challenging aspects of practice teaching, and one that few practice teachers will welcome. It involves breaking bad news to the student, tutor and placement colleagues. Failure means the student's position on the course is deteriorating, and it gives hard-pressed university staff extra work and demands on resources. No one ever wishes to see a student fail, and the process of doing so can be made more difficult by the knowledge of what it may mean for the student. It can involve:

- Loss of career hopes/choices
- Loss of chosen profession
- Loss of self-esteem and image. This can be particularly aggravated in mature students, some of whom, prior to undertaking social work training, are experienced in social work at an unqualified level
- Loss of financial stability. Students make considerable financial sacrifices to undertake training, and may give up employment
- Loss of contact with the student group, tutors, placement colleagues if failure means leaving the course
- Loss of equilibrium; control over life circumstances. It is not unknown for social work students to experience personal difficulties and life-stage crises, whilst they are training. Indeed, these can prevent concentration and contribute to the failure. Practice teachers are often aware of this, and the potential impact on students of yet another area of their life going wrong.

It is therefore not surprising if practice teachers feel uneasy about telling students of impending failure. The loss involved with failure is obvious and the news can trigger a grief reaction for the student, as well as for those connected with him on the placement, on the course and in home life.

Preparing a placement for telling a student about failure

Unease about telling the student about failure can often be intensified by the placement work culture, which reflects the overall success culture of social work education. Roberts (1996) cites Bissell who highlights the image of social work education created by the paucity of its literature on how adult learners respond to impending failure. He considers any realignment of this, to recognise the positives and functional aspects of failure would run counter to trends in the education and workplace, where failure is feared, not discussed, and a 'grin and bear it' approach adopted. It reflects also a success ethic in social work education, social policy and the wider society, with its denial of death, failure and a refusal to recognise ageing.

Long-standing social work aims are ill served by this ethic and can produce a situation where social workers are lined up with their unsuccessful clients against the success-steeped culture of the late 1980s and 1990s Social Service Departments, with their business ethics and jargon.

This culture, with its difficulty in accepting failure amongst established professionals inevitably impacts upon student training. Social workers are also accustomed to an aim of 'caring' so practice teachers can regard the main focus of a placement as that of 'helping' a student to pass it. The assessment of failure can sometimes appear to conflict with this, to the extent that the positive aspects of failure are overlooked. This situation is aggravated if the organisational context is one where success has a high profile, with staff fearing mistakes, and critical repercussions, with no recognition that failure can also represent an opportunity to learn.

Effective work in telling students about failure is also more difficult in the absence of a supervisory framework which values staff contributions and models how to give feedback, addressing both positive and negative practice in regular supervision and appraisal systems.

Work cultures therefore can often reflect a larger societal norm of valuing success, consistent with a competitive society, in which attitudes to failure are punitive. An awareness of this and attempts to counter it, by the creation of a placement culture of acceptance towards failure, forms therefore a useful backdrop to all placements. Few students even when passing a placement do not experience some areas where they feel their practice is weak and disappointing. It is particularly useful where students do fail.

Practice teachers therefore need to address and integrate the prospect of failure in all of the placement planning, and following are some suggestions as to how it can be done.

Pre-placement stage

As part of the preparatory work with the team, a practice teacher should involve them in reflecting on their culture and how they view and respond to failure. This places failure on the agenda right away. It prevents a presumption of success and prevents any tendency to ignore failure as though it is an unmentionable aspect of a work/placement culture. It is important that the placement's line manager is at this discussion, as some existent practices and culture, both of the team and also the broader organisational context may be challenged, with which a practice teacher is not necessarily empowered to deal.

Learning agreement and contract stage

From the start of a placement, the possibility of any student failing as well as passing a placement needs to be recognised. Anything else seems inconsistent with the principles of anti-oppressive practice which should underpin all effective placements. A practice teacher who avoids the issue of failure, could be giving the student a message that she is avoiding the power imbalance and constructive ways of working within it. It is subsequently only fair to students that proper attention is given to the likelihood of failure and effective contract work undertaken. Denial/avoidance or trivialising the potential for failure is unhelpful.

It will inevitably be an issue, even if unspoken for students, so practice teachers should place it on the agenda at the outset, informally and also at the learning agreement meeting stage. If a practice teacher models an open approach to sharing and confronting painful issues a student will be able to share anxieties about failure.

The learning agreement meeting and contract work with students should therefore cover any difficulties identified in the previous placement. A practice teacher should expect to know about these and raise the issue with the tutor and student. She should have access to any previous practice teacher's report. This establishes from the start the climate that difficulties will be addressed. It prevents any attempt by the student to hide such areas, as though they are a cause for shame, or manipulation of the placement to ignore them.

The process for dealing with identification of failure should be attended to at the Learning Agreement Meeting, to the same degree as all other aspects of the placement. It is important to avoid giving it peripheral mention, 'skirting' over the prospect as something rather nasty, for example. 'I'm sure that's not something we want to think about at this stage of the placement, is it?'

At pre-placement and contract stage it is best if a practice teacher is proactive regarding her *attitude* towards failure and *experience* of it. She can state how many students she has supervised and whether they have passed or failed. It is then mentioned in a matter-of-fact way, which helps remove some of the stigma. For example, a statement along the following lines can help:

> I hope you don't fail this placement and I will help you as much as I can. However if I consider your practice incompetent I cannot ignore it. I will however tell you as soon as possible if I think you are likely to fail and whenever possible in time for you to so something about it.

If a practice teacher is an inexperienced or new practice teacher, it is unnecessary to pretend an expertise with students, but she should aim to own her inexperience confidently. Students usually obtain a good service from practice teachers who are in training and have mentor support available. Similarly, new practice teachers are usually experienced social workers nominated by their agency as having the potential to undertake student training, so inexperience as a practice teacher is no cause for apology. A practice teacher can constructively use the fact that she is also being assessed and dealing with anxieties about failure.

Finally, a practice teacher should never, at any stage, advise a student that she will ensure he does not fail, however unlikely it seems. Dealing with failure as one likely placement outcome right from the start, instead of waiting to see if it happens, can be reassuring for all concerned.

Practice teacher profiles

If a practice teacher uses a profile for exchange with a student, at an informal pre-placement discussion, then it is worth including an outline of her experience of failing students and her approach in general towards failure. Acceptance of failure from the early stages of the placement can set the scene effectively for telling the student, if it becomes a reality at a later stage.

Figure 6.1 is a sample profile with suggestions on how failure can be integrated into it.

Box 6.1   Sample practice teacher profile (adapted from Danbury 1994)

1. Personal details
    Name   Ethnic origin
    Any disability

2. Current employment
    Job title   Agency
    Address   Work setting, for example, residential, field
    Client group worked with   Position in hierarchy
    Line manager's name

3. Practice teaching background
    Social work background   Qualifications
    Experience as a practice teacher
    N.B (this section can contain details about the number of placements
    offered and the pass or fail outcome).

4. Practice teacher support system
    (This section can include attendance at workshops, support groups
    and whether the practice teacher is on the Award training and has a
    mentor).

5. Special interests
    (This section can contain particular social work interests which give
    some idea of particular practice methods the student will have the
    opportunity to learn in the placement).

6. Practice teaching style
    General/personal information
    (This section can cover, if a practice teacher wishes, any information
    about her life, family, interest, hobbies, etc.).

Dealing with the student 'grapevine'

It is important for a practice teacher to recognise the impact of failure
amongst the student group, or even previous intakes of students, as the
student 'grapevine' soon operates. A new student then approaches the
placement knowing it is a setting where students fail. It can also occasionally happen that a student on a resit placement can be around when a new
student starts, which brings home even more the realities that failure can

happen. The exaggerated rumours that can abound should never be under-estimated. At placement coordination stage, it is not unknown for students to express a wish not to have a particular placement, because a colleague has failed it previously.

It is therefore particularly important for a practice teacher who has gained a reputation for failing students, to discuss the issue of failure early in the placement with students, and to dispel myths. Placement reputations can often be damaged by rumours from previous students. Highly erroneous tales can be circulated regarding a failed student's experience, who if aggrieved may have presented a biased version. The way of dealing with this is fairly straightforward unless curtailed by circumstances.

If possible, give a new student some information as to the reason for previous students failure. Confidentiality requirements may prevent this, if the students are from the same course and know each other. However, information which can be shared, and tactfully given, can help reduce anxieties in a new student, particularly if, as often happens, the failure was due to a particular circumstance unlikely to reoccur. Sometimes the failure was caused by malpractice and a student new to the placement, if given appropriate information may approve of the failure himself.

If a student resitting a placement is still around, when a new student arrives, involve him in the decision as to what to tell the new student. Much depends on his approach and relationship with the practice teacher. If he is failing his resit placement and likely to be negative and uncooperative, this needs discussion at placement coordination stage. It may be advisable not to accept another student if there is a likelihood of his learning opportunity being restricted because of this.

Selected information tactfully given can often therefore dispel myths and eradicate the ghosts of previous failed students, so placement moves forward.

Personal preparation

As part of placement preparation, a practice teacher needs to develop her own ability to tell a student, if necessary, that he is failing, by reflecting on her own attitudes towards failure, including the advantages as well as disadvantages.

An awareness of the advantages can assist, as it sets the task into perspective and helps contain anxieties in undertaking a task which is already quite complex. If a practice teacher can see no advantages in it for the student then she may feel inadequately prepared.

Practice teachers may approach the prospect of telling the student that he is failing with apprehension, particularly if doing so for the first time. As social workers, they have experience in conveying bad news and communicating with people about areas of their life where they face loss, disappointment, sadness and stress. Similarly they are in a job where they often have to take a hard, unpopular stance, and a tough line telling people what they do not want to hear. The dilemmas between care and control in social work seem transferable to practice teaching, as regards the conflict between support and enabling students and the assessment of failure.

Many practice teachers have considerable skills and training in this area, but initially do not recognise the similarity when dealing with failing students and how their skills adapt to an educational setting. They are also dealing with colleagues and not clients. Students are around in the workplace, so their reaction to the bad news about failure is ever-present, without the distance which can be maintained with clients.

A teaching role can feel less familiar and be imbued with fantasies of a motivated and successful student who provides the practice teacher with some return in the form of mental stimulation, theoretical update and new ideas. Many students fulfil these expectations and provide a practice teacher with job satisfaction. However a minority may challenge practice teachers ideas seriously, so they find it disconcerting to adjust to the reality.

Self-knowledge around expectations of students can therefore be useful preparation work for all placements, particularly when it becomes necessary to tell a student he is failing. It can help prevent the occasional situation where a practice teacher may deny the failure, or collude with the student's bad practice, rather than face the gap between reality and a rigid or idealised preconception about how their student will be.

In preparing to work with students, therefore, it is helpful if practice teachers examine their own attitudes and mental pictures regarding students, as the less they are compatible with the concept of a failing student, the more difficult or surprising the need to tell a student he is failing may be.

Activity 6.1 Stereotypes of students

Content: reflective exercise
Resources: paper and questionnaire
Time needed: 40 minutes

This exercise can be done independently. If done with a group of practice teachers they should work in pairs. The exercise should be completed individually and then shared with a partner. The student profile outlined in the activity can be discussed in the larger group from the perspective of how realistic this student is and how she fits in with their mental pictures of students.

Draw your mental picture of a student on a piece of paper. Write down, without reflection the first adjectives which the word 'student' brings to mind. Complete the following set of expectations. I expect:

- the age of my social work student to be ...
- the previous social work experience of my social work student to be ...
- the sexual orientation of my social work student to be ...
- the commitment of my social work student to be ...
- the financial situation of my social work student to be ...
- the faith of my social work student to be ...
- the political orientation of my social work student to be ...
- the educational background of my student to be ...
- the health, mental and physical, of my social work student to be ...
- the idealism of my social work student to be ...
- the marital status of my student to be ...
- the attitude towards the placement of my social work student to be ...

Include any additional expectations from students.

Reflect on how your picture fits with the profile of a failing student depicted below:

> X is a middle-aged student, and is a single parent. She faces financial difficulty whilst training, so has to work during the course. She has two daughters, one of whom has been accommodated in care and presented very challenging behaviour. X has experience as a home carer and completed an access course to obtain a place on the DipSW, following a general school education with no formal qualification. She fails the placement due to difficulty in identifying oppressive practice, problems in handling power and hostile attitudes to residential social workers.

A remaining area of preparation for a practice teacher is to consider her own experiences of receiving unwelcome news and how it was handled. This can raise awareness of the process and develop the skills in giving negative feedback which are necessary, when preparing to tell a student that he is likely to fail his placement. (Exercise 6.1 at the end of this chapter provides an opportunity to do this.)

When to tell the student

This is largely determined by programme procedures, which usually require a practice teacher to tell the student, as soon as concerns about his practice become apparent. If there is no rapid improvement, then the tutor should be informed and a meeting set up to try and remedy the situation. This may not always be the best time for the student to deal with news of impending failure, dependent on the reason for his incompetent practice. However placement time constraints usually reinforce the need for the student to be told immediately.

A practice teacher can often show an understandable tendency to procrastinate. This is rationalised by a wish to be absolutely sure that there is a difficulty with a student's practice but it can also reflect the practice teacher's anxiety about breaking the news. The task is best confronted as an awareness of impending failure can sometimes provide the student with the necessary stimulus, and becomes a growth point, so his practice improves.

Occasionally a student suspects failure himself and asks a practice teacher whether his progress is satisfactory. In such instances, questions should be answered in an open and honest way. False reassurance or prevarication in order to avoid hurting a student's feelings could be perceived as oppressive and patronising to a student. It would also deprive him of an opportunity to exercise the necessary control over his own learning, and to be involved appropriately in the assessment process, with a chance to make the necessary advance planning and decision regarding his future, should failure become a reality.

How to tell a student

This process can be facilitated, if practice teachers recognise the loss involved for students and themselves in failure, or placement termination, which can happen abruptly with no proper endings. Such situations can precipitate the mourning process in both students and colleagues. The interrelated stages of mourning and griefwork as a response to loss are well known to the social work profession and documented in work done by, for example, Kubler-Ross (1969).

Practice teaching literature does not always recognise that a failing student is involved in the mourning process, as he moves towards the acceptance of a Fail decision. Despite this, the analogies seem fairly obvious, and a practice teacher can usefully consider this when breaking the bad news of failure to all involved in the placement. This process involves various stages.

Recognition of a practice teacher's reaction to the process

Before telling the student, a practice teacher needs to take some time recognising her own feelings about doing so and sharing her anxieties with a mentor if available or colleague. She can often experience a variety of reactions which could be linked to the mourning process:

- Anger – this student should never have been selected on to the course, sent to this placement. I cannot possibly deal with this without more support, less work. I'll never practice teach again
- Guilt and self-blame
- Anxiety – the student/tutor will blame me, appeal against the decision, criticise my practice teaching. It won't help my career
- Depression and sadness
- Relief – I will feel so much better once the student knows.

It is difficult in view of the close working relationship, for a practice teacher not to be sucked in to feeling inappropriate responsibility for the student's failure. Strategies for dealing with these anxieties are needed. For example, it can often help if a practice teacher shares them in advance with colleagues and, if necessary, practices telling the student.

Activity 6.2   Breaking bad news

Content: discussion exercise
Resources: exercise, flipchart paper
Time needed: 45 minutes

This activity focuses on situations where bad news is received and raises awareness of the process of giving and receiving bad news. It helps develop skills in giving negative feedback and sensitivity as to its effects. It can be done as a self-development exercise, with a mentor or ideally in a group of practice teachers working in pairs, and sharing feedback at the end.

The practice(s) teacher should consider the following situations. Select one and identify what your response to it would be:

- a failed examination
- an unexpectedly cancelled holiday
- an unsuccessful job interview.

Think of a situation in your own life where you have failed at something:

- How was the news given to you?
- How did you feel?
- How did you respond?

Scenario

An estate agent has to tell a client that her house sale has fallen through. This house has been on the market for some time. She is now coming to his office to sign the contract. The buyers have announced they are pulling out, due to unexpected redundancy. He could not find the time to ring the woman and tell her in advance. The woman has a young child, her partner is working away, and they want the move to go ahead as soon as possible. She arrives at the office happy, as she has had another pregnancy confirmed. The estate agent chats with her and at the last minute tells her the news. The woman expresses disbelief, then bursts into tears, and tells him they will sue him. The estate agent said he would try to get the buyers to change their mind.

Discussion pointers:

- What do you think of the woman's reaction?
- What do you think of the way the estate agent broke the news?
- How would the woman have felt?
- How would the estate agent have felt?
- If you were the estate agent what would you do?
- If you were the estate agent what would be important to you?
- If you were the woman what would be important to you?
- As a practice teacher what can you learn from this situation?

How to break bad news

When telling a student they have failed, an understanding of the principles of giving negative feedback is essential for the process. Practice teachers can often be effective at giving reassurance and positive feedback, but may need to develop skills in dealing with negatives. Much can depend on their own experience of supervision and staff development.

They also need to understand the assessment process, as evaluative and assessment feedback needs to be distinguished. Advising a student as to possible failure is somewhat different from the feedback process which is ongoing throughout a placement. This gives feedback about performance, with positives and areas for skills development. Assessment feedback has to deal with whether this development is sufficient, within a context of overall competence, and what the assessment decision is going to be.

It is therefore necessary to be clear with the student when feedback heralds failure, rather than being part of the general ongoing evaluative feedback process which occurs throughout the placement.

It can be invaluable for a practice teacher to take some time to practice and think about how to give the feedback before telling the student. This can develop a more confident approach to a student, which in the long run saves a good deal of time and distress for all involved. (Exercise 6.2 at the end of this chapter provides an opportunity to practise skills in giving negative feedback.)

When telling a student about failure, much can depend on the relationship the practice teacher has with the student, and whether there is trust and openness between them. The setting and time is also important. However busy, a practice teacher needs to find sufficient time, in a relaxed setting where the student can be offered privacy without interruptions. She also needs to ensure that he does not have an appointment to rush off to afterwards. Attention to the setting and time availability can help ensure the message is heard and prevent a morass of blame afterwards. Despite all this and however well a practice teacher breaks the news of failure to a student, she should not expect that he has taken it in, and the message may need constant reinforcement. Much depends on the students reaction and how this is dealt with.

Dealing with the student's response

A student's response to news of failure needs recognition and management. It can be affected by several factors, such as whether he already recognises that there are areas of concern about his practice, or whether he suspects, but prefers to avoid the issue.

Alternatively he may be totally oblivious that his practice is dubious or even encouraged to think from a previous placement that it is satisfactory.

Against this background therefore student's reactions can cover a variety of often interrelated stages:

- Shock
- Denial

Telling the student therefore requires a thorough understanding of how to give feedback in a situation where the news is bad. This involves recognizing that it is easy for the person receiving the feedback to feel personally attacked and become defensive. It is not easy to be supportive whilst still maintaining an overall negative assessment position. A knowledge of the ground rules for giving negative feedback and breaking bad news is therefore useful. It is worth a practice teacher taking the time to acquaint herself with these, before telling the student.

Box 6.2   Checklist: The principles of giving feedback

Constructive feedback maintains self-esteem and increased choice. Destructive feedback leaves the recipient feeling bad with nothing to build on.

1. Be specific rather than general
2. Refer to the behaviour rather than the person
3. Be descriptive rather than evaluative
4. Be clear – give one message and in understandable language. Do not give too much information.
5. Check the student's level of awareness about possible failure. Give the feedback promptly, particularly if the student is aware himself that he has made a mistake, for example, mishandled an interview.
6. Come quickly to the point – avoid prevarication in order to alleviate distress. Do not lose the message by accepting how the student may be feeling. This can be dealt with later once the message has been given and received.
7. Recognise the positive aspects, but do not be apologetic about addressing negatives. It is a practice teacher's job to deal with both.
8. Be confident – if a practice teacher 'dumps' on to the student her unease at telling him, uncertainty or anxiety about the feedback this helps no one.
9. Be consistent and check that the feedback has been understood.
10. Give appropriate feedback – link it to the competence and criteria on which the student is being assessed. Do not introduce indicators which are too advanced and have not been shared with the student beforehand.
11. Record the feedback clearly. This ensures that the student knows later what has been said, when he may feel more able to absorb it.
12. Adopt a positive approach to telling a student about failure – it can sometimes be the necessary stimulus which enables the student to move on and redeem the situation

- Anger
- Guilt
- Sadness, depression
- Relief – he thought things were not going well and prefers to know. He was unsure that social work was right for him, so failure makes the decision easier
- Acceptance – the feedback is fair and informed. What can he do about the situation?

A student may experience all of these reactions when dealing with accepting or effectively challenging the fail decision. They represent the task for the practice teacher in dealing with the student's response. This is often the aspect of a failing placement which practice teachers most fear.

It is not, however, all that dissimilar from social work situations where they have to deal with loss and reaction to bad news. The process involves recognising the student's worth as a person and empathising with his distress, accepting the normality of it, including anger toward the practice teacher. The main difference is that the practice teacher is educator and assessor, as opposed to counsellor, and it is usually inappropriate to deal with any personal problems which may have contributed to the failure.

Once the student is advised of the likelihood of failure, then the practice teacher has the responsibility to advise the tutor, and should not leave this to the student. Occasionally students resist their tutor's involvement, fearing a critical response or may want more time to improve their practice, so formal notification to their university can be avoided. However a practice teacher should not collude with this. When involving the tutor, clear focused communication helps. They, like practice teachers, are busy hard-pressed people with resource problems of their own. Tutors can be caught up with similar responses to the practice teacher when they hear about placement difficulties. Even if expected, failure of a student can herald the onset of extra time and emotional demands. A practice teacher needs therefore to take these factors into account when telling the tutor, but they do not justify procrastination. Once the tutor is informed, the failing process is implemented and this involves the practice teacher in recording it and writing the assessment report.

Recording the decision

Current DipSW requirements hopefully prevent the long, rambling narratives which CQSW courses could produce, often written as bland references on the learning process, with little evidence to facilitate assessment. Reports occasionally provided examples of the practice teacher's skills in writing them, rather than any idea of the student's practice.

DipSW requires more structured reports, and evidence for the decision. Each DipSW programme will give guidelines for the specific format for the practice teacher's report, and requirements regarding evidence from the practice teacher and student. Practice teachers therefore need to familiarise themselves with the report requirements:

- All DipSW reports require direct observation of the student's practice. Practice teachers are usually exhorted to refer in their reports to the evidence based upon this assessment method
- The focus of DipSW reports is on the student's competence to practice as a social worker. A student has to pass all competencies in both placements, depending on the programme's terminology – Competent/Not Competent; or Pass/Fail.

Non-assessment of a competence does not constitute failure on the student's part. It reflects on the practice learning opportunities of a placement. It does however require assessment of the student's practice by simulated means, or renegotiation of the practice opportunity in another placement setting. This may involve a placement extension, if the opportunity for some unanticipated reason cannot be found within the practice teacher's work setting. Non-assessment therefore does not mean student failure but it prevents a student moving on to the next placement, or qualifying until this is resolved.

Recording the assessment decision of a placement is an important part of all placements. It involves the practice teacher in gathering evidence of practice from a variety of sources, judging it and compiling an assessment report which gives clear reasons for it. The decision needs to be clear and linked to specific indicators. It should reflect the student's ability to provide evidence of their competence, not the practice teacher's ability to find it and write reports. Reports therefore should contain concrete examples, to justify pass/fail decisions.

It is a potentially litigious situation and a student has a right to appeal against an eventual assessment outcome. An unevidenced report would enable the student to do this, on the grounds that the assessment process had not been properly executed.

It is not always easy for a new practice teacher to feel comfortable with the idea that the Assessment Board may not accept her view as valid, or that the student may challenge it. However, the provision of a full report, with all reasons why she considers the student's practice incompetent in certain areas, can reduce this conflict, as the practice teacher has then done all that can be expected. A well-written report means that, whatever the outcome, she has discharged her responsibility and not compromised her professionalism.

Assessment reports, with their checklists and evidence indicators, can sometimes seem to presume competence and, dependent on the practice curriculum used by the particular DipSW programme, place the onus on the practice teacher to provide the evidence of competence. It is however up to the student to do this, with the practice teacher providing the practice opportunity for the student to do so, and judging the resultant performance. Recording negative feedback and evidence for incompetence can sometimes initially seem to fit uneasily into report structures. These documents often seem based on an expectation that the student presents himself for assessment only when competent, for example: 'The student should demonstrate competence and be able to: support and sustain children and young people ... through the process of change.'

Presenting evidence of incompetence in a framework that focuses on competence can therefore be complex, particularly when students are inevitably competent in some areas. It is important however that ambivalence is not presented and the report is consistent with its recommendation. A Pass recommendation, but evidence that contradicts it, and a long list of identified development areas which belie the Pass, can only lead to confusion and poor assessment practice.

Activity 6.3   Is this report good enough?

Content: discussion exercise
Resources: facilitators, flipchart
Time needed: thirty–forty minutes

This activity can be done independently but ideally with a group of practice teachers working in pairs. Participants should read the report sample and discuss it. They should then share ideas with the whole group and their recorded attempts to rewrite the report.

The practice teacher(s) should read the example below where the evidence belies the recommendation in respect to the level of competence attained.

Competence as an agency worker

Pass overall

X has had to work hard to operate effectively as a team member and has made some progress in understanding procedures and guidelines. Overall however he still has a considerable way to go and I am not sure the necessary progress has been made by the end of the placement. He needs in the next one to give ongoing attention to working within statutory guidelines and to team issues, so that he can develop effective working relations with colleagues, recognising the time pressures upon them.

Reflection points:

- If you received a report from a practice teacher about a student on placement with you, written in this way on several competences, how would you view it?
- What do you think the tutor's response would be to such a report?
- What do you think the outcome would be from the Practice Assessment Panel?
- How do you think the student would perceive this kind of report?
- Try to rewrite this sample of a report, as though it is a Fail recommendation.

Ambivalence about a student's competence can be difficult to record, without invalidating the outcome of competence. However it is possible to distinguish between an overall level of competence, if it is clear that skills development within a basically competent position is needed. For example:

Overall student X has shown competence in contributing to the management of care. I base my judgement on direct observation of him, when working with Case 2. He was working with a woman newly discharged from psychiatric hospital, with no friends or support network. He undertook an initial housing assessment and ... these examples confirm my view that he is overall competent at a sufficient level to develop networking skills, when it is necessary to advocate on behalf of the client. Within this overall position of competence X still needs to develop in ....

When failing a student a practice teacher should be able to accredit competence to the student, where appropriate, without concern that this will then invalidate the overall evidence for incompetence. The main issue is that the practice teacher provides clear examples of the poor practice which has given the cause for concern. Writing the report reflects the stage of the placement when the assessment decision has been made.

It is not good practice in report writing to reflect the self-doubts and questioning which have been part of the process leading up to that decision. Present the evidence of the student's practice and the reasons for the judgement made, and then leave it up to others involved in the assessment process to make the final decision.

Programmes which include self-assessment schedules from the student or examples of the student's evidence can assist here. If a programme does not allow for this, then a practice teacher can always include 'live' evidence of a student's practice, as this then has not been filtered by her judgement. (Exercise 6.3 at the end of this chapter provides an example of a Fail report and an opportunity to practice writing them.)

Once a Fail seems likely, a student should be given a plan which outlines the competences which constitute the difficulty, and what the student has to do to produce the necessary evidence of competent practice. It is useful if a practice teacher includes this also in her report, alongside comment as to progress on it, and the eventual outcome.

The student should have full access to the report; a chance to comment upon it, and, if he disagrees with the outcome, to give reasons for this. Writing Fail reports is not easy, but meticulous recording is well worth the time involved. It is important to remember that the readers of the report have no knowledge of the situation, so it is best to err on the side of stating the obvious. It is also important to ensure that the process is clear, and that the Fail procedures have been implemented and at what stage in the placement.

Some programmes will ask a practice teacher to state what she thinks the assessment outcome should be as regarding the student being allowed a repeat placement. This is not easy and needs reflection around issues such as:

- Is the student a dangerous practitioner, likely to cause emotional or physical harm to service users? If so, reasons for this need to be given
- At what stage in the placement did the practice which caused the failure occur? Did the student have a chance to learn from it and remedy it?
- What is the student's response to supervision about his poor practice? Will he accept it, use support and supervision? Recognise mistakes and be open about them.

Once the student is told that he has failed the placement and been given a written report to this effect, then hopefully he will accept this decision, or at least tolerate it until the final decision of the Assessment Board, when he can consider his options. However this does not always happen and problems can develop within placements which fail students. In either event, work with failing students can be stressful and a practice teacher needs to consider her own support needs.

Exercise 6.1   Role play on giving feedback

Content: role play exercise
Resources: facilitator, scenarios
Time needed: one hour

The aims of this exercise are to:

- Provide an opportunity to practice giving feedback in a fail situation
- Develop assessment skills and evidencing feedback.

The exercise should be done with a group of practice teachers, working in groups of three: one participant in the role of practice teacher, one in the role of student and one in the role of observer. The following scenarios should be given to all three.

Scenario one

A practice teacher has concerns about a male student on his first placement. These concerns are shared by colleagues. The practice teacher has missed two supervision sessions, due to illness and unexpected court attendance. On return to the office, a colleague reports that the student has made sexist jokes to a member of the administrative staff. The practice teacher is already concerned about the student's oppressive attitudes to female service users, but has, as yet, found this difficult to pinpoint, with tangible examples. She undertakes direct observation of the student's practice. He interviews a client whose husband is away. During this process, he suggests jokingly that she has been having a bit of fun whilst she is off the leash. The client laughs uneasily at this comment. Afterwards the practice teacher challenges this practice. The student tells her his comment was a joke – to establish rapport. He insists that he is from working-class origins and knows the culture and how these people carry on, the kind of banter they use, with no offence intended or taken.

Role play

The three participants should, in role, enact a practice tutorial, at which the practice teacher feeds back on the direct observation and expresses concern about the student's practice. Interim evaluation is near, so she intends to share the concern with the university tutor and to 'flag' up this placement as a potential failure. The student expresses shock and denies any awareness of difficulties.

After the role play, the observer should feedback on the process of the tutorial and the participants can share ideas on this. This exercise can be videoed, so it can be viewed and discussed afterwards. It can also be set to role play situations where the feedback is poorly given, and then after discussion, re-enacted with an attempt to improve it.

Exercise 6.2   *Practice in giving feedback*

Content: discussion and role play
Resources: facilitators, examples lists, flipchart
Time needed: one hour

The aim of this exercise is to:

- Provide an opportunity to develop skills in giving feedback
- Provide an opportunity for reflection on the ground rules for giving feedback.

This exercise is designed for a group of practice teachers who should work in small groups. Each small group should brainstorm on to a flipchart ideas as to ground rules for giving feedback. The larger group should then share these and identify common principles which should be listed. Each small group should then consider some of the examples listed below, as to how the principles of giving feedback can be applied.

They should then be asked to each write down an example of poor student practice which can be taken from 'live' situations in their experience. These can be distributed amongst the groups randomly. The group task is to prepare a statement giving an example of how this could be raised assertively with a student and an example of how not to address it. This exercise can be completed in one workshop or two, with a gap in between. It can also be augmented with role plays of some situations where the feedback is given to the student.

Examples list

- 'You were right to tell the nurse it is our job to assess residential care and its not her decision, but I think she felt put down and her opinion not valued.' *Rather than:* 'You seem overbearing to other professionals'

- 'She seemed upset when you suggested she clean up her house. She may have felt you disapproved of her and subsequently felt intimidated about talking to you.' *Rather than*: 'Your way of talking to people about their housekeeping standards is not good'

- 'I thought your aim was to be helpful and reassuring when you told X that the information she gave you was totally confidential to you, but it would have been fairer to tell her that realistically it belongs to this Agency which you represent. It would have prevented future difficulties for you. You need to read up on our policies on this.' *Rather than*: 'You should not have given Mrs X the promise of secrecy with information she imparted to you. This breaches Departmental policy and code of practice'

- 'I was concerned to hear you congratulate X that her pregnancy is beginning to show, so you expect that she will be giving up work soon. Such remarks are sexist – I do not think she appreciated it. As an administrative assistant she is a valued member of this team, but she is young and inexperienced and may not have felt able to assert herself. Do you think your remark was appropriate?' *Rather than*: 'You should not have made that remark to X. It is sexist and highly inappropriate in an office setting and makes me doubt whether you can practice in an anti-oppressive way consistent with our principles in this Agency.'

Exercise 6.3   Report writing

Content: discussion exercise
Resources: facilitators, report excerpts
Time needed: 40 minutes

The aim of this exercise is to:

- Develop skills in writing fail reports.

This exercise is best done with a group of practice teachers who should work in pairs and consider the following report. They should discuss it and then share ideas on it afterwards with the whole group. This exercise can also be done independently, or shared with a mentor.

Report excerpts

Develop professional competence
Use supervision effectively, agree priorities and manage own work schedule.

X was unused to supervision. Her experience of it was that it would be used punitively and only if she fell down on her performance. We agreed a supervisory function which included support, educative and assessment components and a contract which included the use of an agenda. Although unused to drafting an agenda, X showed willingness and progress in formulating one. However, she was never able to use it and only on two occasions prepared work in advance as agreed. She seemed very inhibited by the power imbalance in our relationship and unable to assert herself when she felt her workload was too much. She advised her tutor of this instead. X also had difficulty in juggling college, work and home demands. She relied on me excessively to work out a plan for her but was not able to keep to it. She was unable to keep one client contact because she had forgotten about a change in her college timetable and she left a message on my answerphone to say that she would not be in. She did not negotiate out of her meeting but had forgotten about it. This meant colleagues had to remember and fill gaps for her. It was part of her values system that broken appointments should be explained to service users. She completed an exercise on planning priorities which showed an ability to do this but she was unable to implement it.

Discussion points

- Adequacy/inadequacy of this report: practice teachers should attempt to rewrite areas they are not happy with
- Is the Fail recommendation appropriate for a first placement?
- Is the practice teacher expecting too much?

7   The support needs of practice teachers

Finding a way round the support system

Students inevitably need support when faced with failure and the loss and grief associated with it. Similarly practice teachers have support needs, if they are to facilitate the Fail process for students. Their needs usually involve the following areas:

- Emotional support
- Support with assessment – a sounding-board to check out their judgement
- Assistance with implementing procedures.

When dealing with failure – and the event can happen suddenly – practice teachers need to know about the kinds of support and monitoring available to them, and to access quickly the appropriate source for the specific difficulty. Few practice teachers who have failed a student describe the process in terms other than stressful and emotionally demanding, even when the Fail is obviously in the interest of all involved.

Practice teachers' anxieties about failing a student

A practice teacher's aim for a placement is rarely to fail a student, so this outcome can produce much soul-searching, focused around various concerns:

119

- Is it me? Could more time/experience/skill have got the student through?
- Is my judgement sound? Am I too subjective, expecting too much?
- Have I been oppressive? Is my judgement inadvertently affected by racism, sexism homophobia, etc.
- Will my student cope with failure? What will it do to him?
- Will the student disagree the decision? Appeal? What does this mean?
- Are my teaching skills sufficient?

Conversely a practice teacher who has passed a borderline student about whom she still has concerns may have similar worries. Practice teaching is responsible work, so if the teacher passes a student about whom she has doubts, she may feel her professional credibility is on the line, particularly when a student is going to a colleague within the same organisation for a next placement, or applying for employment within the same agency.

There may always be an element of reality in some of these doubts, as given enough time, help and a chance to resit placements, all except a minority of students might get through. However, assessment requirements impose a cut-off and expect a student to practice competently within time constraints. Practice teachers therefore have to deal with the dilemmas and conflicts involved in failing students. The need for professional support in such situations therefore seems obvious. Its provision is in the interest of both students and practice teachers.

Indeed there should be a wide range of support systems available to practice teachers. If they work in an agency approved by CCETSW for the provision of practice learning, then there should be established systems for support, training and the provision of time in which to undertake practice teaching. A practice teacher in an approved agency should be made aware of the support available by her training section.

Practice teachers need however to know where it is appropriate to take a particular difficulty about a placement, and the kind of help to expect from the different sources. This can depend on the problem and the help needed.

Line manager

A practice teacher's line manager has responsibility for the overall super-vision of the DipSW placement. Many organisations which provide place-ments are now part of a partnership, and have a service level agreement with a DipSW programme. Placement provision should therefore be part of a team's service delivery and as such on the managerial agenda, integrated with output to service users. Regretfully, some line managers may still regard practice teaching as peripheral to a team's work, leaving it up to a practice teacher if she wants to do it.

Similarly, some line managers are not practice teachers themselves, so cannot advise on all aspects of the practice teaching function. Despite this, an interested line manager can be an invaluable source of support, particularly with the emotional demands a failing student can make, and has expertise to transfer from similar situations in staff supervision.

There are some clear formal and procedural areas for line managers' support and involvement:

- The negotiation/agreement to accept a student on placement
- Integration of the placement within the workload management of the team and provision of time for the practice teacher
- Practice teacher absence through unexpected illness or work commitments requires a line manager to give attention to the student's placement needs.

A line manager does not have the assessment responsibility for the placement, but can be involved in giving feedback. He or she therefore can convey an opinion to the practice teacher as to the student's competence and readiness to practice, but cannot overrule the practice teacher's decision. This is a somewhat atypical situation in respect to the normal accountability arrangements for a practice teacher's social work. It can be a potential source for conflict, although it is unlikely that a practice teacher will not consider seriously feedback from a line manager, who has experience of appointing and supervising qualified staff, about a student's suitability to practice social work.

Line managers are also involved in practice teacher selection. This usually involves their nominating practice teachers to the training section of their organisation, as suitable to undertake student training. They also have to recommend them for award training and agency approval. This involves both references, and in some instances, a formal assessment report on their practice teaching competence. The line manager therefore has a quality control function regarding the practice teacher's work. He or she should be involved in an agency's monitoring procedures for the quality of placements and receive feedback from the placement evaluations completed by many programmes at the end of the placement.

The line manager can therefore be involved in the feedback process to the practice teacher on the quality of her work and would certainly have a role if the practice teacher's work was poor. The line manager's monitoring function should provide a source of protection for a student against poor-quality practice teaching.

Ideally, a line manager will support and oversee all placements and their progress as a regular part of their staff and supervision function. Performance as a practice teacher should also be part of staff appraisal and this part of the appraisal can be done in conjunction with an agency's training section, and Practice Assessment Panel (PAP) feedback on the quality of the practice teacher report.

Students who fail their placements can however pose specific situations which require managerial involvement and is distinctive from other placements:

- A complaint may be made about the student's practice which, when investigated, proves valid, and requires reparation work with service users or other agency workers
- A student may need suspension from a placement for misconduct or malpractice
- A student may become mentally or physically ill and require an absence from a placement. In extreme and unusual situations a student may not accept this, yet cannot be regarded as safe to work with service users or be around the placement
- A student may invoke complaints procedures against a practice teacher or other work colleagues. This is not specific to failing students only, but they are more likely to feel aggrieved.

The situations outlined above are unusual and may prove beyond the capacity of the practice teacher to manage on her own, whether experienced or not. They need managerial involvement, to implement agency policies and assist with the liaison with the university and the implementation of their procedures also when relevant.

Tutor

The input of the university tutor in placements where the student is failing is essential, and many practice teachers regard the support of the tutor as invaluable in such circumstances. DipSW programmes and Accreditation of Practice Teachers and Agencies has begun to see a variety of differing patterns regarding tutor contact and support to placements, which has traditionally been two or three placement visits during its duration.

Much attention and emphasis has been placed on improving practice teaching to promote high-quality placements, but much less on the role of academic staff in this process, for whom there is no similar accreditation process and status. CCETSW (1996) comments, *Assuring Quality for Practice Teaching*, merely expects tutors to ensure that students and practice teachers are clear which practice requirements require special attention in final placement, and assessment, and to be involved in double marking academic work related to practice. Paper 30 (1995) similarly refers merely to recommendations for double marking and some involvement in intermediate and final assessment.

Arrangements can therefore vary from programme to programme, and the tutor's role is usually clarified in practice teacher handbooks. It is therefore useful if a practice teacher acquaints herself with the way each educational establishment organises its tutorial arrangements, and develops links with the appropriate university staff.

A personal tutor is the member of university staff with particular responsibility for each individual student. Again arrangements can vary amongst programmes in respect to arrangements for placement support. One tutor does not always see a student through the entire course, but a different one can take over at mid-point. Similarly the responsibility for placement finding and coordination and placement monitoring and management may be divided between different tutors. This can lead to a disjointed system which needs careful clarification to practice teachers and students so they are clear with whom they need to liaise.

Placement shortages have resulted in their coordination often becoming tightly managed by agency training sections. This has replaced the direct contact and placement arrangements by tutors, who developed personal contact with specific practice teachers, so they formed ideas as to which students might suit specific placement requirements and need a particular practice teacher's style and expertise. There were some advantages in this arrangements which may be lost with tighter agency coordination of placements, and the reduced role of the tutor in placement finding.

However accreditation requirements now mean more specialisation of practice teaching. Service-level agreements and 'ringfencing' of placements, although regrettable, may mean a gradual development of a group of practice teachers familiar with a specific DipSW programme. Hopefully, this will create effective bridging between university and placements, as well as links between tutors and practice teachers when they need to work in partnership.

Within this context, the tutor to the student on placement has a specific function:

- Pre-placement work with the student on his placement request and to assist the student formulate his learning needs, in order to demonstrate competence, and where appropriate, to identify his specific pathway for the course

- Participate in programme preparation workshops with agency staff
- Participate in and often facilitate the Learning Agreement Meeting at the beginning of the placement
- Participate in mid-point review to evaluate a student's progress
- Monitoring of the quality of placements – this can involve participation in a final placement evaluation meeting, although all programmes do not hold these.

A tutor has the more general role also of managing and maintaining the nature and amount of information available to the practice teacher about the student as regards to his academic and personal life.

Tutors also participate in various ways in PAP membership and the appraisal of practice teachers' reports. A tutor reference for a practice teacher is also needed, at application stage for agency accreditation and some award programmes also require this endorsement of a practice teacher's competence.

In respect to situations where the student is at risk of failure, tutors have a formal and often increased role. This also applies to placement breakdown or termination. Most programmes require tutor involvement at any stage of the placement when failure seems likely. In such situations the tutor has a specific role to:

- Support the student. A tutor may identify if a practice teacher is expecting too much of a student, or if he is the victim of a collusive work culture which is unable to accommodate any challenge or difference which a student presents
- Participate, with the practice teacher, in devising a plan for the student which identifies competences which are not met, and help the student understand what he needs to do to try and satisfy requirements before the end of the placement
- Share with the student's knowledge, and ideally agreement, any appropriate details regarding the student's academic progress, university performance, which might inform or assist with the student's progress on the placement
- Advise the student, using knowledge of the Credit Accumulation and Transfer Scheme (CATs) of other courses which might be available for transfer should placement failure seem inevitable.

As well as specific Fail situations, a tutor who is involved with a placement may have a more general support and facilitative role. In the event of a personality clash between a student and a practice teacher, the tutor may try to facilitate, to the extent at least of determining whether it is practicable for the placement to continue.

A tutor also has a support role to the student in the event of the placement's failure to deliver. For example, if a practice teacher is off sick and no student supervision is offered in her absence, the tutor may need to advocate on the student's behalf with the agency. Similarly the tutor will also be advised if the student is involved in agency complaints procedures or malpractice.

It is also not unknown for a tutor to be able to identify a situation where the student seems to be progressing satisfactorily, but the practice teacher and student are colluding on avoiding areas of weakness. A tutor may attempt to facilitate in these situations, or can terminate the placement.

Many practice teachers and tutors might consider that they need regular contact if they are to adopt the training team approach to a placement, on which this outline of a tutor's role is based. However, some DipSW programmes over the past few years have seen a reduction in tutor contact, and formal placement visits can range from three to none. In the latter instances, a university representative will usually come out to the placement, if difficulties are indicated.

The rationale for reduced tutor/placement contact is usually pressure on tutor resources. The recent rapid expansion of student training has changed many of the traditional relationships between students and tutors, as academic staff have larger numbers of students, which can reduce individual access. Reduction in placement contact can however also reflect the view that agency and practice teacher accreditation developments has shifted the balance between university and agency, so regular contact is needed less. Practice teacher training and agency infrastructure for placements has increased to replace some of the support and induction of inexperienced practice teachers which was traditionally provided by tutors with CQSW.

Some programmes therefore consider that the traditional pattern as regards tutor contact can change, freeing up tutor time for more effective use within the student's overall learning and development. However many practice teachers have themselves been educated and trained within a traditional tutorial system of individual support and placement back-up, which they regard as essential support to themselves as practice teacher and a necessary source to students This can be seen as applying particularly to Fail situations, where students can feel very disempowered, without regular university contact throughout the placement.

It is useful therefore if a practice teacher clarifies her views on this important issue of frequency of tutor contact.

Activity 7.1   Tutor's visit to a placement

Content: role play discussion
Resources: facilitators, flipchart
Time needed: one hour

This activity aims to focus practice teachers' thinking on the role of the tutor in placements and whether there is a need for regular placement visits and the best use of tutor time when placements are in process. This activity is designed for a group of practice teachers who should work in small groups of three. Each small group participant should adopt the role of tutor, student and practice teacher. Each group should spend 25–30 minutes discussing in role the following issues:

- What role should the tutor take during the placement? If the word 'support' is used, this should be defined
- Does the tutor need to visit the placement if all is going well? If yes, how many times?
- Some programmes do not make formal visits to placements unless there are problems. A written mid-placement evaluation is requested. How can the placement be managed in this situation? What alternative use could be made of the tutor time as placement back-up?

Each group should summarise the main points of their discussion on to the flipchart and then discuss their perspective with the whole group.

Placements Co-ordinator

All DipSW programmes have placements co-ordination systems. Since Agency Accreditation started, many have designated training officers/senior practice teachers to undertake this function, as well as the supporting and monitoring of placement development. They usually also maintain close links with the university involved in the programme partnership and with the tutor or administrator designated to find placements.

Training staff who have responsibility for placement development can consequently adopt a support role. This arrangement can sometimes be formalised, for example in a 'long arm' arrangement with new practice teachers who are gaining experience prior to commencing award training. Accredited and experienced practice teachers may use training staff on a consultative basis for support, generally with placement or specific difficulties.

Approved agencies should make information regarding support arrangements clear to their practice teachers. Consultation can be on an informal basis and can cover a variety of issues.

Change of placement setting

Sometimes, as a placement progresses, there are insufficient learning opportunities available, or the student presents a particular learning need. It may subsequently become necessary for the student to undertake some work in another setting, as part of a placement 'package'. Practice teachers may make these arrangements themselves informally, but consultation with the placements coordinator can assist. He or she can provide ideas as to settings and has an oversight of a range of placements and their occupancy level. This can mean the best source of the learning opportunity is identified for the student, integrated within placement demands as a whole.

Personality clashes

The placements co-ordinator can sometimes facilitate if personality clashes occur between student and practice teacher. The student often refers this to his tutor, and the practice teacher may wish to seek advice from within the agency, from a person who is more distanced from the placement than her line manager.

This situation sometimes involves the acknowledgement and resolution of transference feelings by student and practice teacher. This is well documented in Danbury (1994), and refers to situations where a practice teacher may become anxious, if she recognises that her response to a student may lead her to dislike or feel indulgent, because of a previous relationship or situation which stirs up feelings inappropriate to the student. A practice teacher may be used to working like this with service users, but not always in an educational setting. These transference feelings can affect the teaching relationship if unrecognised or not used constructively. Acknowledging them with an experienced practice teacher from the same agency can assist, particularly in the area of expectations and standards for the student's assessment. Often practice teachers feel concerned that their relationship with the student is a close one, and lacks objectivity so that transference can affect assessment adversely.

A senior practice teacher who has a broad range of experience across a variety of students and courses and who is outside the placement, can prove a useful sounding-board and can facilitate the development of strategies which are teaching rather than therapy-orientated, where students are also carrying inappropriate agendas from previous relationships or educational experiences into the placement.

Assessments and troubleshooting

Training staff can also be consulted on assessment issues, regarding realistic expectations of students, validity of evidence and the quality of a practice teacher's report. In addition, training section placements coordinator can also be contacted about any difficulties with a university, regarding, for example, tutors not visiting when needed or lack of information. Sometimes a practice teacher can negotiate independently about these matters, but a training officer's involvement can take the pressure off busy practice teachers. Some of these issues reflect on the quality of the placement. Agencies are represented on programme management groups and thus can have a formal monitoring and management role regarding them.

Providing support

Placements coordinators can be usefully involved in placement termination and suspensions as they can advise on the realities of alternative placement for students, and prevent inappropriate pressure being put on a practice teacher to carry on with a placement because it will be difficult for the student to find another.

They can also advise on procedures when a student fails a placement and can provide support to a practice teacher through them, particularly in respect to any Assessment Board attendance. A few training sections pay for workload relief or overtime for practice teachers and as such provide a major resource function to a placement, as well as an overall responsibility for monitoring the quality of the placement.

Mentors

In order to become Accredited, practice teachers now have to attain the Practice Teacher's Award. This means an increasing number have the support of mentors whilst they gain experience of taking DipSW students on placement. The concept of the mentor derives from the ideas of an experienced person providing advice to others, usually in the same professional activity. The mentor therefore provides:

1. Support for the development of the practice teacher's skills and professional identity.
2. Education, that is, help with understanding and applying the academic basis of practice teaching such as models of adult learning, teaching methods.
3. Assessment of practice teachers' competence: a mentor is usually an experienced practice teacher, whose role is distinct from that of a line manager. As part of their assessment function they need, in order to meet CCETSW requirements for the Award to:

   - Directly observe the practice teacher supervising a student
   - Provide feedback on a video of a practice teaching session
   - Liaise with the student and the line manager on the placement progress and its practice teaching
   - Prepare a mentor's report as part of the portfolio the practice teacher presents for assessment in order to attain the Award.

The mentor therefore can be a major source of support to a beginning and inexperienced practice teacher. Mentors have influence on a placement and facilitates decisions regarding the student, though the power to make the Pass/Fail decision remains with the practice teacher. Practice teachers undertaking Award training are relatively inexperienced, so the situation where a student fails the placement can be stressful and a mentor's support can prove invaluable in several areas:

- Help with the assessment decision: the mentor can act as a sounding-board regarding this and provide advice regarding standards and realistic expectations
- Appraisal of the video of a practice teaching session and other evidence of a student's practice. The mentor can act as an informal second opinion and can give feedback on the practice teacher's skills and whether these are affecting the process
- Assist with the development of strategies to assist with a student's development
- Facilitate with incompatibility between a practice teacher or student
- Assist in the identification of practice teacher collusion or denial of student poor practice, and discuss ways of dealing with this, rather than inappropriate assessment decisions
- Liaise with the placement managers in an advocacy role if a placement meets resource difficulties, or the practice teacher's training, to which an agency makes a commitment, is jeopardised by resource difficulties.

Practice teacher workshops

Peer supports are invaluable with most placements, but particularly ones where a student may fail. It is particularly essential where a practice teacher is working in an isolated setting, which is her only work setting. Most programmes provide workshops as a part of the placement process. Some agency training sections also provide regular practice teacher development meetings. Practice teachers from the voluntary sector whose organisations are too small to maintain them can usually negotiate in to any workshops and meetings run by their local social services department, particularly if they are taking students from the DipSW programme with which it is in partnership. These groups have various advantages:

- They provide an essential arena for sharing anxieties about judgements of a student's practice, as well as providing an opportunity to sound out views regarding minimal standards and share expertise in the assessment of failure. In a low failure culture, practice teachers have few models of this. If doubts about a student's practice are shared, a group of practice teachers can provide useful differing perspectives
- Video recordings of a student's practice, if rendered suitably anonymous, can be shared so that practice teacher groups can provide a useful source of second opinion, which can either reinforce a practice teacher's opinion in a way which builds confidence or change it.

The use of colleague workshops as a source of support with failing students involves a practice teacher in sharing her anxieties and her practice This requires a safe environment. Workshops can therefore also have disadvantages:

- Workshops can have a constantly changing membership, so they become topic focused, with little chance for the climate to develop which is needed for sharing practice
- Confidentiality is essential but can be difficult to maintain, particularly in small agencies where the practice teacher network is small. This can inhibit free discussion
- A new practice teacher can find the experience of others daunting, particularly if very experienced practice teachers use the workshop to 'play to the gallery' in a setting where a safe atmosphere is not established, with the group working as a team
- Difficulties in sharing anxieties and practice can occur, if a colleague

is in the group who has already had the student on placement and passed him.

Award Course Training

The practice teacher groups which are cohesive enough to provide the kinds of support needed by practice teachers who are encountering difficulties with students, can often be found on programmes which run Award training. This involves the same group of practice teachers meeting over a period of time, with skilled facilitation available. The group can come from a number of different Agencies which allows for a variety of different perspectives and practice teaching experience.

Independent counsellor

Programmes can vary as to the extent to which they can make available counselling help to students for practical and emotional difficulties. It is worth considering the appropriateness of using counsellors at the point when students fail. This process can involve the student in grief work, and sometimes in an appeal against the assessment decision. It is usually inappropriate for tutors and practice teachers to combine their assessment role with supporting the student through the mourning which their decision has precipitated. Such a situation produces a role conflict which is stressful for a practice teacher. An independent counsellor can therefore be an invaluable source of support to the student and placement.

Outside facilitation might also prove useful for a placement if the line manager's normal support systems prove inadequate, or if they are not geared to work with the effects of failure and loss in an educational situation.

'Buddy'

A practice teacher who has concerns about a student's practice can look for support from another practice teacher colleague on an informal basis. This constitutes peer consultation and can have many advantages. The 'buddy':

- Provides a safe environment and is particularly helpful when the 'buddy' has had experience of failing students. Specialist practice teachers who work regularly with a group of students often build up this experience and can contribute to the development of less experienced colleagues through this system

- Reduces the isolation of some practice teachers. Generally, failing a student can prove a lonely experience even when working in a team, if colleagues have not also experienced the process.

The arrangement can however also have disadvantages:

- Practice teachers will inevitably select colleagues with whom they feel safe, have similar views and ways of working which can lead to collusion
- There may be resource problems, as consulting with a 'buddy' needs time to be effective and often is best done outside a practice teacher's work setting.

There is some value in the training section coordinating the 'buddy' arrangements to ensure it is set up and agreed: when faced with the Fail crisis, it puts extra pressure for a practice teacher to negotiate this much needed support.

Second opinion

Programmes which have opted to utilise second opinions can provide invaluable support to practice teachers:

- Practice teachers feel the decision regarding fail is not all left up to them
- The process can be fairer to students.

However, seeking a second opinion has disadvantages:

- Resource and coordination problems
- Practice teachers can find it threatening, particularly if they disagree with the person providing the second opinion as to who may have more experience
- Students may attempt to sabotage the process or manipulate the two practice teachers destructively. They may see it as part of a complaints process in respect of the practice teacher skills.

Consultants

Most DipSW programmes will have expectations that black students have support groups available, as well as consultants, if they are placed with white practice teachers in predominantly white placements. Some agencies will also aim to provide the white practice teachers with the same facility. Consultancy should not absolve practice teachers or agencies from pursuing anti-racist practice policies and training. Also ideally it should be available to all practice teachers offering placements, as a corrective to the assumption that only placements with black students need consultancy, or that black practice teachers offer the solutions to all training for black students. If all agencies tackle racism and offer good supervision and support, consultancy would not be needed to plug the gaps.

However, given the current reality, most DipSW programmes need to make consultancy arrangements for black students with practice teachers, so that black students have placements on equal terms with their white colleagues. It is useful therefore if practice teachers have an understanding of the function, so they can use consultancy effectively and decide if they are prepared to take a black student on placement without it.

It is essential that consultant support is available from the start of the placement, so he or she is not brought in to 'troubleshoot' when it faces difficulties. It can be valuable for a practice teacher to have access to a consultant when support and advice on cultural issues are needed. The consultant can act as a sounding-board on assessment issues, to aid recognition of the perspective from which a judgement is made. For example, the skills and experience of a black student may not always be fully understood from a white perspective, if it denies or is uninformed about what is good practice in the student's culture.

Similarly a consultant external to a placement may be able to identify situations where a student fails inappropriately, because a work setting denies racism, so is not open to challenge about it.

Failing a black student or any member of a disadvantaged group can be difficult for a practice teacher, as it arouses anxieties about her judgement and whether it will be regarded as oppressive. It can be tempting for a white practice teacher to avoid failing a black student. Properly established consultancy can help offset this form of racism. It can in fact sometimes encourage the practice teacher in her judgement, as a consultant can give feedback which reinforces her judgement, and counters any assertion by a student that his practice is being misjudged because his culture is misunderstood.

Once the failing process is under way the consultant's view on how to support the student effectively can be invaluable, particularly an awareness of how failure is viewed in the student's culture and how loss is handled.

Box 7.1   Sample model for a black consultancy to a placement –
guidelines for an agreement

Some programmes will expect the practice teacher to have regular sessions with the consultant. Others may appoint one to be available as required and leave the use optional for both practice teacher and student:

- Consultancy must be resourced and in place at the placement start. It should be coordinated by the programme and not left to students to find
- Consultant should be independent from both course and agency
- Student and practice teacher can have the same or different consultants, but if using the same one, then separate sessions should be offered
- Consultant(s) should attend the Learning Agreement Meeting. The time availability needs resourcing. One recommended guide is eight hours per student and eight hours for the practice teacher plus travel costs
- Consultant should safeguard confidentiality, but cannot give absolute guarantees
- Consultant has a supportive role to the placement. They will therefore advise and mediate on issues arising from the placement
- Consultant should participate in the assessment of the student only to the extent of giving feedback to the practice teacher
- Consultant will provide feedback to the programme on the curriculum and to the agency on policy and procedures
- Consultant's role may include advocacy on issues arising from the placement. They assist with checking out policy and put practice into context, allowing for any discriminatory practice to be challenged.

It could be argued that a consultant should be available to all placements which take students from any disadvantaged groups which might encounter oppression. However this is seldom organised formally, but left to practice teachers to make informal arrangements with colleagues, dependent on their understanding of the values of the role. In situations where it is used a consultancy needs careful negotiation, role clarification, with effective contract work at the start of the placement. A consultant is only likely to work effectively where this spadework has been done, and where the practice teacher has addressed the issues of oppression and established a safe assessment climate.

Failing a student is a situation where a practice teacher is most likely to need to use the support systems available to her. Asking for help and owning up to problems is not always easy. It is however expected of students and a practice teacher should be able to model a positive approach to this and some facility at doing it. This requires a knowledge of what support is needed for a particular problem and the most appropriate source, as well as skills in actually asking for it. (Exercises 7.1 at the end of this chapter provide role plays and scenarios to develop expertise in doing this.)

Activity 7.2   What do I do?

Content: self-development exercise
Resources: copy of exercise
Time needed: 30 minutes

This activity is a self-development exercise which can be done independently by a practice teacher or shared with a mentor on completion. It raises awareness of support which might be needed and about asking for help.

The practice teacher should consider the following:

- When taking a DipSW student on placement what is my existing support system?
- What support might I need which is not available?
- How easy do I find it to ask for help? To trust those who help me? Think of a situation where you have asked for help. List in the box below three things you found easy about this:

```



```

List in the box below three things you found difficult about this:

```



```

- How assertive can I be if I request help and it is not forthcoming?
- When working with a failing student which aspect of the process would I need most help with?

Activity 7.3   Maze of support

Content: self-development exercise
Resources needed: copies of maze, paper, blue and red pencils
Time needed: 30 minutes

This activity assists a practice teacher to identify the support systems needed for work with a failing student.

P.T.
Workshops   Video equipment   'Buddy'

             Tutor   Admin support

Workload management   Time

                                      Second opinion

          Agency handbook

Placements coordinator   Mentor

                                           Consultant

             Office space

       Colleagues   P.T. handbook

          Supervision room   Award course

Line manager

On a piece of paper, list in blue the support in the maze which is available to you as a practice teacher. List in red the support in the maze which is not available to you on a scale from 1–5, with 5 being the least available.

Consider what you can do to try and ensure the missing support is provided. Start with the numbers at the lowest end of the scale.

Plot the path through the maze for a practice teacher who is wanting to tell a student that his practice is unsatisfactory. The student is avoiding supervision. He has already said that he is not satisfied with its quality and is referring this to his tutor. Where should the practice teacher go with this?

In this situation what support would you need which would not be available to you?

Ground rules for seeking support external to the placement

At most Learning Agreement Meetings, attention is given to where to go if there are problems, although this can be understated and referred to in very general terms. Procedures usually need detailed clarification as the need to use them arises. A student can often, if reacting to the shock of being told about potential failure, need them explained again and will look to the practice teacher to guide him through the process. A practice teacher needs therefore to:

- Re-state the procedures if failure is likely
- Establish that a student has the right to take issues of concern about the placement to his tutor and to seek support from his university
- Establish that a practice teacher also has a right to support and supervision. This is formalised in mentor work and similar ground rules are valid for other sources of support
- Total confidentiality can never be agreed with a student as ethical issues affecting good professional practice and safety cannot be kept secret. If this ground rule has not been established in the early stages of a placement, it needs to be, if failure is likely and support external to the placement is sought. (Exercise 7.2 at the end of this chapter provides a discussion exercise on ground rules.)

Practice teachers do not necessarily need support with all placements, but when they do, it can apply to any regardless of whether the student passes or fails. They need therefore a thorough understanding of their support system. Problems can develop in all placements and the likelihood of this can be increased in those which attempt to fail students.

Exercise 7.1   Discussion: What do I do?

Content: discussion exercises
Resources needed: copies of scenarios
Time needed: one and a half hours

The aims of this exercise are to:

- Increase knowledge of when to use the support system
- Develop skills in using it
- Promote discussion on ground rules practice teachers need to estab-
  lish with students.

This exercise can be done with a group of practice teachers who should
work in small groups. They should consider one or both of the following
scenarios, as selected by the workshop facilitator, dependent on its purpose
and length. The groups can discuss the scenarios in line with the pointers
included, as well as any other issues they identify. The small groups can
then feedback to the whole group. This exercise can be varied by discussing
real-life scenarios which practice teachers bring to the group, or by asking
each small group to think up a scenario which can then be passed round for
the others to discuss.

Scenario A – stage one

You are a male practice teacher and have Paulette on her first placement.
From the start Paulette has been ill at ease. She finds it difficult to communicate directly and confidently with you. You have tried to be reassuring,
build trust, but little progress has been made. You are now getting concerned as to whether Paulette has sufficient skills in working with service
users in areas where she might need to deal with hostility, use power or
challenge others. You have tried role play to develop her skills, but her
difficulty in maintaining eye contact led to concerns about her ability to
engage with people. A female colleague tells you that Paulette has confided
in her the information that her marriage broke down shortly before the
course started. Your colleague did not have Paulette's permission to share
this with you, but she is also concerned about her.

Interim evaluation is due. The programme with which you are working
does not have a tutor visit for this, but asks you to write an interim report
on placement progress. Whilst you are wondering what to do, you undertake a joint visit with your student. A service user confronts her angrily
about an issue. Paulette diverts the discussion to a non-contentious subject

and placates him. In discussion afterwards Paulette agrees she did not respond well, but blames it on the fact that she is under a lot of pressure with college. There are positives in Paulette's practice, as she is able to work with females and children who are dependent on her in a supportive and empathic way.

Discussion points

- What should you do?
- Which sources of support should you contact?
- What sources of support should be available?

Scenario A – stage two

You decide to discuss your concerns with Paulette's tutor. You tell Paulette of your intention and the areas of her practice about which you have concern. She does not disagree with your judgement. The course centre is some distance away but the tutor agrees to come out to the placement. He advises you that Paulette has problems, for which she is receiving counselling. This information was not shared with you before, as the tutor was concerned about breaching confidentiality. The tutor also tells you that Paulette has recently been to see her and told her that she cannot perform properly on placement because she finds you oppressive, and direct observation of practice inhibits her. The tutor is unable to get to the meeting as arranged. Another one is fixed up but Paulette goes off sick. Time is now getting short, as the placement is well over the half-way stage.

Discussion points

- What do you do now?
- Who else might you need to involve from your support network?

Scenario B

You are Mary, a student on a final placement in a residential unit for people with a learning disability. Your practice teacher, Heather, is the unit manager and she is very busy. You have been given plenty of practice opportunity on the placement and have been directly observed several times, by a senior care worker who gave feedback. At interim stage, Heather expressed satisfaction with your progress. However, it was acknowledged that she had not given much formal supervision, although you were able to talk together informally occasionally. It was agreed at the meeting that she would need to improve on this. Heather then went on a course for a week and the situation on her return got worse as she was so busy. You are becoming concerned about the lack of supervision and loss of learning opportunities. You respect Heather's abilities and think she has much to offer you. Another direct observation is needed to meet assessment requirements. Your tutor at the interim evaluation meeting had made it clear that two of these must be done directly by Heather to meet assessment requirements. You are getting worried as to how you are going to pass the placement in the time left, and whether Heather can complete your report. Heather assures you that you will pass but can give no indication as to how the time problem will be resolved.

Discussion points

- What can Mary do?
- What issues are involved for student if:
  - they complain about lack of supervision?
  - suggest the validity of a practice teacher's report must be affected by lack of supervision?
  - indicate officially that their learning opportunity has been inadequate?

Scenario C

You are Joe and run an adolescent unit. Your student is Mark. He is a mature student with pre-course experience in voluntary work. You have had concerns about his practice but have given him the benefit of the doubt. This is his first placement and you think it is sufficient to identify areas for further development. These are around values. Mark is organised, efficient and writes excellent reports and the young people quite like him. He has however a difficulty in working with the team, as he considers that its approach is too lenient and that insufficient discipline is maintained. You personally have had some difficulty working with Mark – his political views which he states around the unit quite dogmatically are different and he is strongly religious. You suspect he is intolerant of others' views but he has concealed this. He is fully aware of what social work values are and has behaved in accordance them so far. You are worried that in your assessment you may have been too lenient because you are uneasy about disliking him.

You have had to be firm that no physical sanctions can be used against children, and discussed with Mark fully the unit's policy regarding control. Mark has adhered to this until shortly before the end of the placement, when he smacks a child once across her backside. The child incurs no physical damage but is very upset.

Discussion points

- What do you do?
- Who is it necessary to involve?
- What policy and procedures have to be implemented?

Exercise 7.2   Ground rules when support is needed

Content: discussion exercise
Resources needed: facilitators, copies of scenario
Time needed: 30–40 minutes

The aim of this exercise is to:

- Develop expertise in using the support system
- Promote discussion on the ground rules practice teachers need to establish with students.

This exercise is designed to be done with a group of practice teachers working in small groups. Each group should discuss the scenario outlined and then feed back to the large group.

Scenario

You are a practice teacher and have a final placement student. He is a non-graduate entrant who worked as a home carer before the course. He returned to education in his late thirties after little formal education. You get on well with your student. His practice is good particularly in the area of interpersonal skills. He struggles academically and never believed he could attain a Higher Education qualification but is hard-working and determined. Towards the end of the placement you notice he is looking very stressed. He says it is because he works weekends to make ends meet financially. He also shares with you the fact that his partner has recently been diagnosed HIV-positive and this is causing real pressure at home. Because of your own professional background you notice signs of drug taking. Your student confesses that he is dependent on them and is receiving help to come off them. He assumes that you will keep this confidential and says the last person he wants to know about his difficulties is his university tutor whom he claims to dislike and finds patronising. You share this view of the tutor.

Discussion points:

- What should you do?
- Can this be ignored? What message would it give to the student?
- Where can you go within your agency to discuss this?
- What is your agency's policy about illegal drug use amongst staff?
- What ground rules should you have established with your student about confidentiality?
- Do you have to contact the tutor?

8 Problems in placements

Problems in managing failing placements

There is a dearth in the literature on practice teaching about failing students, and the difficulties which can generally occur in placements and which need careful management. Ideally once a student is advised that failure is likely, he will engage openly with his practice teacher in discussion of her feedback, and will provide fresh evidence, if he disagrees with her judgement of his practice. The placement can then proceed to one of the several possible satisfactory outcomes:

- The student develops the necessary competence and passes the placement
- The student accepts the Fail decision and makes alternative career choices
- The student disagrees the decision and makes an appeal, using correct procedures and both understanding and having appropriate grounds for this
- The student is offered a repeat placement by the Assessment Board.

Unfortunately this is not always the situation, and once a student is advised of potential failure, problems can develop which make the process anything other than smooth. Some are specific to failing placements. Others can affect placements, but are aggravated in Fail situations.

Practice teachers, when commencing work with students, may not always be prepared for encountering difficulties in placements. This is sometimes influenced by their own experience as students. A practice teacher may have had a very satisfying learning situation herself whilst a student, and her motivation to practice teach stems from a desire to re-create this for her own students. Similarly she may have experienced placements as a disappointing, or even disastrous part of her own training. This can lead to a wish, when undertaking student training herself, to ensure that students find placements a positive experience which is not upsetting or miserable.

Often the initial placements a practice teacher offers can reinforce the positive experience of her own student days, or help her compensate for their deficiencies. Placements which present difficulties can be a negative process for both practice teacher and student and can therefore involve some considerable adjustment and disappointment initially.

The task of dealing with problems on placement can be facilitated if practice teachers have the opportunity, at a fairly early stage of their training, to reflect on what problems they may encounter, and to address some of them in simulations.

Before considering the kinds of difficulties which can arise in placements, it is also useful, if a practice teacher thinks through in advance some of her expectations regarding students.

Activity 8.1   Expectations regarding students on placement

Content: self development exercise
Resources needed: copies of exercise, flipchart paper
Time needed: 40 minutes

This self-development exercise aims to help practice teachers develop awareness regarding their expectations of students and their potential for presenting difficulties on placement. It can be done independently by practice teachers. On completion, it could be shared with a mentor. It could also be done with a group of practice teachers working in pairs, with issues arising from it being shared by the whole group at the end.

1. How did you experience your own placement when a student? Answer this separately for both placements if you wish.

1	2	3	4	5

    Horrendous   Excellent

2. I expect my student's motivation to learn to be:

1	2	3	4	5

    Very high   Very low

3. I expect that whilst on the placement the likelihood of my student experiencing marital, personal, family difficulties will be:

1	2	3	4	5

Inevitable   Nil

4. I expect that my student want help from me with difficulties over managing the course academically:

1	2	3	4	5

Inevitably   Never

5. I expect that my student, in respect to having a criminal record should have:

1	2	3	4	5

None at all   One that can
                                                      be disregarded

6. I expect my student will be resourced so that financial problems affect the placement:

1	2	3	4	5

Not at all   Make
                                                     continuation
                                                      impossible

7. I expect that my student's pre-course social work experience will be:

1	2	3	4	5

None   Extensive

8. I expect that my student's pre-course formal academic level will be:

1	2	3	4	5

Graduate   A Level   None

9. I expect that my student's choice over his placement will be:

1	2	3	4	5

Absolutely   A broad choice
none

10. I expect that my student's contact with SSD as a service user will be:

1	2	3	4	5

- -

Never   My student's
                                                                                             children are on
                                                                                             the CP register

11. I expect that my student's main objective in wanting to become a social worker is to:

1	2	3	4	5

- -

Improve the   Get off Social
   world   Security benefit

Add up your score and decide whether it indicates that you are idealistic or cynical regarding your expectations of social work students. Scores ranging towards 1 equate with idealistic. Scores ranging towards 5 indicate cynicism.

How prepared are you for problems? Make a list of the kinds of problems you think students could present on placement.

Activity 8.1 can give a practice teacher some insight into whether her expectations regarding students are realistic, and include a recognition of the potential for problems on placements, other than those involved with helping students through the learning process. The transition from a practitioner role to that of a teacher of practice, and of enabling students rather than service users, is not always an easy transition. An entry into the world of training involves the acquisition of some new expertise. The kinds of problems they can encounter with placements, particularly ones associated with failing students is not something that practice teachers automatically expect. However, social workers are accustomed to problem solving and therefore have a good basis for transferring these skills to a less familiar educational setting, once they recognise the need to do so. This can only be done once the kinds of difficulties which can occur are recognised.

Students can refuse to accept a Fail decision by a practice teacher

Milner and O'Bryne (1986) recognise a trend for social work students to be notoriously difficult to fail, and to resist accepting a Fail decision. This can particularly apply if they are experienced students. The reasons for this are several:

- Students may be experienced as unqualified social workers or in voluntary work, or are already established and qualified in related professions, seeking career change or retraining following early retirement
- Students may be sponsored for training by their organisation, often the same one as the practice teacher works for, and with jobs to return to
- Students have often made real personal and financial sacrifices in order to undertake social work training and therefore taken risks of which they are not fully aware at application stage.

Failing a student on practice grounds can therefore get messy and emotionally fraught, carrying a threat of appeal, even litigation from the student. A younger student with little pre-course experience may find it easier to accept and move on to choose an alternative career, before irreversible decisions are made. The situation can be more difficult for experienced students.

Academic failure can also sometimes be more acceptable, as students come from an educational background where examinations and assignments have to be passed. It also seems more distanced, whereas failure in the helping professions can give particular hurt to students, where practice involves interpersonal skills and values. Failure in this area can sometimes be more difficult for a student to accept, as he may perceive it as his failure as a human being, involving insensitivity, inadequacy and the inability to form relationships.

Once failure is likely, a student often stays on in the placement and on the course, whilst the decision is ratified, and the future outcome for the student decided. This period can cause difficulties, the student may experience:

- Shock and denial, and in its more extreme form a student may not believe that failure is likely. He may behave as though he has not been told, or appear bewildered when he is given the record of the meeting which discussed his failing performance. He may need additional reinforcement and a restating of the concerns about his practice, and extra support to sustain him through a painful process
- Depression, which can occasionally be severe and needs an attentive approach from the placement. Suicide threats are rare but not to be totally unexpected
- Anger, which can sometimes take the form of a defensive attack on the practice teacher's own practice or skills. The evidence for failure is often based on judgement and perception. A student can decide his

practice is as good as his practice teacher's, and refuse to accept the decision. He may argue that it is the practice teacher's judgement which is at fault not his practice, or that too much has been expected. Threats of appeal are common and anger can be displaced on to other parts of the programme

- Guilt and blame – inadequacy feelings on the part of the student can be projected on to all involved. Students who are failing placements can be adept at ensuring the practice teacher, if not the entire placement staff, feel responsible emotionally for their failure. Similarly they may blame families for lack of support.

Occasionally a student who fails a placement does not complete it but leaves abruptly. This means a placement loses its student without endings and disengagement being possible. It can leave the placement feeling bereft, let down or inadequate.

The distress can be not just the student's but that of the whole placement whose staff have vested time and effort into it, with success the hoped-for outcome. The placement therefore loses its happy, appreciative student who has benefited from the learning opportunity they have provided. Milner and O'Bryne (1986) cite Parke's work on the mourning process, where he describes how the loss of a member of any social unit can create a situation where a whole group, even when a few members are affected more, becomes anxious, restive and potentially defensive. This can apply to a placement group. Colleagues on it will have their feelings about any experience of failure or fears of it reawakened. Other students on the placement can find the failure of one of their peers triggers their own anxieties about it on this or future placements.

The failing student, if resisting the decision, may exploit this situation, for example by complaining to peers, seeking out colleagues, the practice teacher's line manager and service users to advocate on his behalf; he may use positive comments from other sources to challenge the practice teacher's assessment.

The whole team may look to the practice teacher to 'pick up the pieces' in this situation, where grief counselling may in fact be needed, although it is not always recognised as such. Similarly, the student who is failing may turn to his practice teacher for support and counselling, with the emotional and practical problems that the failure has created for him. Constant proximity in the placement makes some level of emotional engagement between the practice teacher and student inevitable. The need to support students through traumas affecting their service users' lives can also sometimes mean that emotional support is of paramount importance, and supersedes the need to focus on areas where the student's practice needs improvement. All this can make for a difficult environment in a failing situation.

A practice teacher who is failing a student can also find herself under impossible pressure to model constantly good practice herself, particularly if a student is resentful of her judgement of his practice. He may be looking for weaknesses in hers, so he can counter that she cannot herself demonstrate competence in areas where she is criticising his practice.

The situations outlined here are not easy – they are inevitably stressful for a practice teacher to handle, combined with the relentless pressure of a social work job. They should not be regarded as applying to all failing situations, but represent perhaps the worst scenario, and also some of the understated anxieties that practice teachers can have about working with failing students. They need addressing by agencies and the profession if it is not to opt out of effective practice teaching.

In order to resolve some of these difficulties a practice teacher needs to develop strategies for containing them. She needs, for example, to think carefully around her role and its boundaries. Conflict will inevitably occur when her supportive role involves sustaining a student through the failing process. Unless this is resolved, a practice teacher may be left with self-doubts, and a reluctance ever to practice teach again if it means having to fail a student.

It is very difficult without undue stress for a practice teacher to combine a support/counsellor role with that of the assessor who has created the crisis for the student by failing him. Unlike many losses experienced, it is not one totally out of the control of the practice teacher. It is the direct result of her professional judgement and if she could be prevailed upon to change her mind, then some of the difficulty for the student would go away.

Similarly, if she attempts to counsel the student on difficulties, either practical or emotional, which may have impeded his progress on the placement, then she is at risk of losing objectivity as an assessor. She could also be open to the student saying that she has ignored mitigating factors, when they are irrelevant to the assessment, or that she knows so much about his personal problems that she is biased and punitive towards him in his student role.

A structure needs to be found for working with this situation. A practice teacher should identify her own sources of support and give a high priority to finding the time to use them. She may need to involve her own line manager in this, but it is important that her anxieties are contained.

It may be necessary to call a meeting of the university tutor, the placement line manager and the student to identify the difficulties the failure is giving the student and how these can be resolved. It is usually helpful to acknowledge the distress that failure can cause, and the normality and inevitability of the student's feelings. If the student needs help with the emotional or practical difficulties produced by the failure, then he may need to be offered referral elsewhere. The tutor may be able to access through the university student counselling services and external independent counsellor who can undertake:

- Loss and grief counselling
- Personal counselling
- Career advice
- Financial and debt counselling
- Advocacy in an Appeals process.

Picking up the pieces in the placement after the student has left can also be difficult, particularly if the student left with bad feeling and a complaint in process, or threats of Appeal pending. The need for external support for students is particularly recognised by Borrill (1991) and Milner and O'Bryne (1986), as is also the inappropriateness of leaving it to a practice teacher to deal with the placement's reaction. Failure, loss of team members and its effects is not specific only to student placements, but it is also a part of teamwork and staff development. Normal line manager support systems can often therefore be sufficient for dealing with this situation. However, if the team has found the placement particularly stressful, it can be helpful if an external facilitator is brought in to work with them as a whole on reconstruction after a failed placement. (Exercise 8.1 at the end of this chapter outlines some problem situations in fail placements and provides a chance to devise action plans for their resolution.)

Tutor contact

The input of the university tutor usually proves invaluable in placements where students are failing. The tutor can support both student and practice teacher and undertake a key role in resolving problems in a placement. The role of the tutor and its changing nature, in some programmes, has already been identified in Chapter 7 – the focus here is when problems occur in the contact. These may be more likely to happen in situations where a university representative only comes to the placement when difficulties are 'flagged' up, and is therefore unknown to the practice teacher and sometimes unfamiliar to the student. This can be an uneasy situation for all concerned, and can reinforce any tendency by the student, and perhaps even the practice teacher, to see the tutor as an omnipotent figure who will adjudicate in the situation or apportion blame.

Danbury (1994) outlines the difficulties which can occur when a practice teacher is anxious about her teaching ability. If this goes unrecognised it can lead to a 'splitting' of the university and the practice setting by both student and practice teacher. The student may attribute to the tutor an expert role and an inexperienced practice teacher may be tempted to collude with this, and feel she is being assessed also. She may be tempted to adopt a student-like dependency role if her own training is recent, deferring to the tutor's judgement and seeking validation of her own. The tutor's visit therefore may resolve or exacerbate this situation and the resolution of it is particularly important in fail situations

Tutors, like practice teachers, may find the prospect of a student failing emotionally demanding. They face the loss of the student from their group and the course, or the pressures of finding an alternative placement for a student. It is not unusual for tutors to have been involved in the selection process for the student, and to feel responsible for taking on a student whose suitability for social work is subsequently challenged. Although it is unrealistic, students can attempt to manipulate them on this basis.

The tutor therefore can become a depository for the student's stress, despondency about failure and complaints about the practice teacher and the placement, which can create a pressure to counsel, adjudicate and to advocate on behalf of the student. Often the tutor can agree with the practice teacher's concerns but, if not, still needs to maintain a supportive approach to the practice teacher, or at least one which recognises her credibility as a co-trainer. This is a difficult balance for tutors to maintain, and is a potentially conflictual one of which a practice teacher needs to be aware, and the kinds of difficulties it can occasionally create:

- Tutor may collude with the student, denies difficulties; implies the practice teacher's standards may be too high and regards academic progress as the paramount factor
- Tutor gives the impression that alternative placements are very difficult to find, and that this should be a factor in a placement assessment decision
- Tutor or assigned university representative does not respond to the request for a placement visit to discuss difficulties; takes too long a time over doing it, or has a sudden illness or unexpected time demands which necessitates appointments being broken
- Contact with the tutor can shift the power imbalance inappropriately. The tutor's role is facilitative, but the practice teacher has the assess-

ment responsibility, although sometimes the tutor is more experienced as a trainer
● Occasionally friction can develop between the tutor and practice teacher, as the roles can overlap and it is a potentially rivalrous situation. This is particularly open to destructive manipulation by a student, especially when time resources and constraints exist.

A practice teacher needs to be prepared for these situations even though not the norm, so that she can develop strategies for dealing with them.

Procedure when a tutor does not respond to an indication of difficulties

If a tutor does not respond when placement difficulties are indicated, then the practice teacher must pursue this and insist on a university representative meeting with her, particularly if it is part of a programme's assessment requirements. It may be necessary to write formally, and to involve those accountable at the university and agency for placement provision – it is not appropriate for the student to take the role of message carrier. In extreme situations it may be necessary to state that the placement must be suspended if the tutor input cannot be provided. A practice teacher may need the backup of her agency for this. This is a tough line to take, particularly if the tutor's absence is due to illness or the kinds of pressure that practice teachers, as colleagues, can understand. However, it is in the interest of good assessment practice and for the protection of the student that the tutor function is provided.

A real pressure in this situation is that of time and a practice teacher can feel constrained to sort the situation out herself. This leaves her vulnerable to student complaints, or with insufficient time to undertake the failing process in a caring and sensitive way, whilst carrying alone and inappropriately the responsibility. In this situation she may need to seek facilitation and support elsewhere whilst waiting for the university to respond, so her anxieties can be contained, if the placement is to remain student focused.

Difficulties between the practice teacher and tutor can usually be resolved by an open discussion, as long as time pressures are not used as a means of avoidance. Once again an inexperienced practice teacher may need to mobilise her own support systems within the Agency in order to effect this. Occasionally some discussion may need to occur without the student being present, so the practice teacher and tutor can function as part of a teaching team, sharing ideas as to how to resolve a student's difficulties.

It is not uncommon for both social work trainers and students to believe that a student has a right to be included in all contact between practice teacher and tutor, but this cannot always work as in the instances already described. Just as a student sees his tutor and practice teacher on his own, so may they may need to assert the same freedom. Ideally boundaries regarding this should be laid down at contract stage, so the student is clear from the placement onset. The tutor and practice teacher may need to assert their right to meet independently, but can advise the student that if his behaviour and progress are discussed in his absence, they will aim not to say anything behind his back, which cannot be said to his face.

Placement shortages

The relentless pressure on placement resources can create various difficulties for practice teachers:

- Late starts or insufficient pre-placement planning time
- Delay in obtaining information about students – profiles, details of a programme's curriculum, handbook
- Resentful students who did not request or want the placement but were told it was the only option. They may seem set to be resentful throughout the placement, so that learning is affected.

A practice teacher needs to weigh up these situations carefully, and consider her response to them. She can be left feeling that the student has been 'dumped' upon her, so she is left carrying inappropriately the strain of placement shortages. In such a situation, relationships between agency and university can soon spiral downwards negatively.

Similarly, hurried placement starts, without adequate information in advance, can create difficulties for practice teachers, particularly with failing students. It can mean she lacks the time for thorough assessment, so the student could challenge her decision, or a practice teacher be left with insufficient time for a borderline student so she passes him, although uneasy about this. It is the practice teacher's name that accompanies the assessment decision in all placements, so she can feel her professional credibility is jeopardised through insufficient time to plan a placement. A practice teacher needs therefore to take action to resolve the difficulties this may cause.

Strategies to deal with the difficulties of placement shortages

A practice teacher can decide to accept the situation. If she is already familiar with the Programme and an experienced practice teacher, then a hurried start can sometimes be accommodated. Placement shortages are beyond the control of everyone and a practice teacher will not wish to make the situation unnecessarily worse.

She can insist on a later start to allow for adequate planning time, or a placement extension for the same purpose. The assertion of the right for sufficient planning time can cause difficulties with university time-tables Students can also be anxious and angry about such a situation. The situation needs careful evaluation but a practice teacher should insist on the provision of adequate planning time if good practice requires it.

The reluctant student needs thorough consideration before a practice teacher agrees to accept him on placement. Practice teachers are not always aware of how much the placement shortage impacts on students' lack of choice. Students can be told there is only one placement available and it must be accepted. This disempowers them in the pre-placement discussion, as they lack the same freedom as practice teachers to discuss and mutually decide whether it is appropriate to the student's learning needs.

Often, once a student meets a practice teacher and the placement, his resistance disappears, but if a practice teacher considers the placement really will not provide the kind of social work experience he wants for his career aspirations and learning needs, she should back him up. Obviously placement shortages obviate against this being done lightly or for frivolous reasons.

Similarly, if a practice teacher considers a placement could meet the student's learning needs but his resistance is so great, and irresolvable that it will impede his progress, then she may have to refuse to accept him. A student who is all set to resent being on a specific placement, can create a destructive learning experience for all involved. Both practice teacher and placement colleagues will inevitably experience it as a rejection of their service user group and a devaluing of their placement, and it will form an additional and unnecessary pressure on all involved.

Malpractice

Malpractice by a student can cause obvious difficulties for a practice teacher in the management of the placement, as it can usually involve the suspension of a placement whilst the situation is investigated by the agency. If unfounded, then consideration will be given to the placement continuing, which creates pressure on time-scales at both the university end and for the practice teacher's workload and planning.

The kinds of behaviour recognised as malpractice can also be stressful for practice teachers to deal with, particularly if unused to staff or student supervision. They may be accustomed to it in service users but the transition to dealing with it in the work setting, where the student's presence can inhibit free discussion, is not easy. It assists if the practice teacher has a clear understanding of the definition of malpractice, and actions to be followed in the event of an allegation which integrates agency and university procedures. (Box 8.1 at the end of this chapter outlines one such procedure.)

The kind of behaviour which is regarded as malpractice can range from dishonesty, drug addiction or drunkenness in the work setting, to abuse of service users or breach of confidentiality. Although certainly an unexpected and infrequent occurrence in a placement, practice teachers can be alarmed when it occurs.

It is not unknown for them to feel very angry at having to deal with malpractice, expressing the view that programme selection procedures should be such that students likely to present such behaviour should not be accepted. Similarly, they may think that the programme should have mechanisms for identifying students, who are subsequently found to be unsuitable off the course, *before* the placement starts. This often stems from concern for service users and a reluctance to see them exposed to inappropriate student behaviour, and used as training fodder when practice is unacceptable. This attitude is understandable but avoids the reality that once a student is on the course, it is inevitable that unsatisfactory practice can only be fully identified and assessed on placement. It will inevitably fall to the placement to eliminate it and this is much of what DipSW partnerships are about.

Much as the profession should strive to maintain high selection standards, it lacks infallible systems for never selecting or qualifying unsuitable social workers – any child abuse situation involving a qualified worker makes that regrettably clear. Placements will need to continue playing a major role in identifying and eliminating malpractice and its resultant problems. If a practice teacher considers the issue of malpractice from qualified staff and the even greater impact this could have on service users, then this can assist with the development of a positive attitude to the need for vigilance and to dealing with such instances, hopefully small, amongst students.

When practice teaching arrangements break down

Occasionally a practice teacher's illness, family situation or workload crises may necessitate her being away from a placement unexpectedly. Hopefully, a placement is accepted as part of service delivery, so that at the Learning Agreement Meeting a colleague has been identified as a back-up in the event of the practice teacher's absence. Other team members, as long as they are qualified social workers, can provide back-up in the situation of unexpected absence of the practice teacher. In a setting where there is only one practice teacher, then the agency placements co-ordinator may have to be contacted, to discuss alternative arrangements, such as another placement or 'long arm' practice teacher support.

Where these arrangements are not in force, or in a voluntary sector placement where there is only one practice teacher, then the tutor needs to be contacted, so the student's progress and continuation on the placement can be considered.

Ideally, it is in the interests of an Agency which wants well-trained recruits to manage the situation where practice teachers are away from the placement. If they do not, then a practice teacher could return from an absence to find her own workload is presenting a considerable backlog, and the student has received minimal supervision. This can mean a student is at risk of having a non-assessed placement outcome. This is not a Fail situation but the effect is that the student cannot continue on to the next placement. This will cause the student anxiety, and emotionally it may feel the same to him as failure. In such a situation a practice teacher may have no alternative other than to notify the university of the situation and request a meeting with the tutor so that a placement extension is considered.

Once again real pressure from the university and the student can exist to finish in time, but the practice teacher even though sensitive to the student's difficulties, may have to take a firm stance on this. This kind of situation can leave the practice teacher often carrying feelings of failure and guilt, which are unrealistic. As regards good assessment however, it is not viable for a practice teacher to turn a placement which is non-assessed because of time constraints into one where a student is shuffled through and the evidence made up.

Practice teachers need however to be aware of the options available, so the difficulties are brought out into the open and the responsibility for dealing with them shared. It is particularly important not to neglect discussing the student's feelings about this. Intellectually, he may be able to understand and sympathise with the reasons for his practice teacher's absence, and recognise that they are outside anyone's control, but emotionally the student may still feel abandoned and resentful that he has been left unsupported. Recognition and acceptance of this by the practice teacher can assist and support the student through the difficulties of an extended placement, which can increase financial pressure and impose upon family and vacation work plans.

Placement extension/suspension/termination

An extended placement is one where a student continues a placement after its intended end, in the same workplace and usually with the same practice teacher, in order to demonstrate competences which have not been evidenced in the number of days required. Placement extensions can be agreed in a variety of situations:

- Illness or absence from the placement by practice teacher or student
- A student is assessed as having difficulty with one area of competence which a short extension of the placement would address.
- A student needs to stay on in the placements a bit longer for an appropriate practice opportunity to be found, for example, a service user may have refused to cooperate or died, so the appropriate learning opportunity has unexpectedly not been available.

A suspended placement is where a placement ends before the required number of placement days have been completed. They can also be agreed in various circumstances, some of which dovetail with extensions:

- Investigations of alleged student malpractice
- Investigations of a complaint by the student about the placement. If these complaints prove unfounded then a student may return to the placement and it is extended to allow the necessary placement days to be completed
- A placement can be ended by the tutor, student or practice teacher. This usually occurs in situations such as incompatibility between student and practice teacher; or an inability of the agency to maintain the placement so that the student's learning needs are met. Sometimes in the situation of the practice teacher's unexpected absence, an agency may suspend that placement to provide an alternative one.

Whatever the precipitating factors, placement extensions and suspensions can be difficult, as they often are a response to unexpected factors and expensive on scarce placement resources. The anxiety as to whether an alternative placement can be found is often a major factor with tutors and students, and this can often become a pressure on practice teachers to continue the placement. This can prevent the best decision for the student's learning being made, or else the decision is delayed until the placement has reached a crisis and broken down completely.

Extended placements beyond the time originally expected can create planning difficulties for a practice teacher whose workload may not adjust easily to the student staying on longer than expected. They can also mean the extension runs into the arrival of new students, with concomitant over-crowding and an exhaustion factor for the placement. These factors need to be taken into account by a practice teacher when agreeing to an extension, and above all it needs resourcing so the decision should be taken in con-junction with her line manager and, where relevant, the placement coordinator.

Placement suspensions can mean the student leaves the placement sud-denly, so the placement is faced with the need for rapid disengagement and adjustment to the loss of its student. The practice teacher needs therefore to develop a strategy for dealing with these unusual placement endings. She needs to:

- Identify her own support needs and the appropriate person to help
- Handle the transfer with service users. It is particularly important to be vigilant for any tendency of a student to blame service users for placement difficulties which have led to the placement suspension and to take it out on them. Service users need to be given appropriate information as to the reasons why the student has left, so they feel exonerated from any responsibility. Also they need the opportunity to express their response to the student's sudden departure, as they may have liked or become dependent on the student
- Encourage the student wherever possible to say goodbye to colleagues and service users
- Discuss with the team the placement suspension and share reasons wherever possible and feelings about this. Hopefully this enables disengagement and helps the team to regard the process as an occa-sionally inevitable part of student training, so that they move on towards acceptance. Otherwise a team can get stuck, feeling resentful, inadequate and resistant to ever taking students again.

Repeat placements

These are not always problematic, but can be different and complex place-ments, so practice teachers need to be clear concerning the commitment they are undertaking, when agreeing to provide a student with a repeat placement. Often these placements are provided by specialist practice teachers or practice learning centres where agencies have them. However, the implementation of accreditation requirements has seen the creation of a better-trained practice teacher group. It is not at all unusual for 'singleton' practice teacher to be asked to take students who have been offered an opportunity to resit a placement by the Assessment Board.

Repeat placements are always the result of formal procedures which include the Practice Assessment Panel (PAP), sometimes a second opinion and the Assessment Board. There is often a significant delay between the original placement and the start of the new one. This is to allow assessment processes to be implemented, but also reflects the pressure on placements and the fact that it is not easy to find practice teachers who are willing and resourced to provide them. This means students have often undergone a period of anxiety up to the Assessment Board and then over where they can go for the repeat placement.

There is a wide range of requirements for repeat placements regarding their time, length and whether only some or all competences need reassess-ing. They do however mean that a practice teacher knows that a student has had difficulties in a first placement, so that it had been failed or sus-pended. Students can therefore present a range of different situations in respect to placement repeats:

- Student accepts the Fail decision and recognises his areas for devel-opment and is willing/able to address them
- Student arrives blaming the failure on the first practice teacher and placement's oppressive style. This can seem realistic sometimes. It can also create anxiety that this is what the student will say about any other placement which fails them
- Student arrives with a practice teachers report which may place the responsibility for the failure clearly on the student
- Student has been allowed a repeat placement only because of a suc-cessful appeal against an Assessment Board's decision
- Student may arrive with a practice teacher's report which indicates a thorough assessment was undertaken in a previous placement, and a clearly evidenced Fail decision. The Assessment Board may give no indication why a repeat placement was resultantly agreed and what the expectations are regarding a repeat placement.

It is worth a practice teacher taking the time to consider and discuss thoroughly with the student and his tutor the kinds of uncertainty these situations can create, and in advance of the placement starting. It is advisable not to be pressurised into hurrying or bypassing pre-placement discussion and planning by any time shortage presented by university timetable and deadlines. Although time restraints are important concerns for any student, they should not be a reason for taking shortcuts on clarifying expectations and learning needs, as this can reduce anxiety and save time once the placement starts.

It is particularly important to consider the student's approach to the placement in order to establish boundaries and ensure he can work with a second practice teacher. Students may bring to a repeat placement emotional baggage from their first. It is not unusual for them to show:

- Resentment over the failure. This may have caused financial and family pressures
- Low confidence and esteem. They may feel stigma is attached to failure and be embarrassed about placement colleagues knowing the situation
- A distrustful attitude to a new practice teacher.

Students may arrive wishing to tell a new practice teacher how awful the previous one was and they may try to manipulate a new practice teacher into promising to get them through. It can be tempting to fall into a rescuer role.

In addition, the practice teacher may know the previous practice teacher and placement. Careful consideration needs to be given as to whether the repeat placement is viable in this situation, particularly if there is any danger of the student coming with negative preconceptions having been already formed in the second placement. It is essential that the new practice teacher feels free to make a reassessment and come to an impartial decision, without it creating conflict with a previous placement

Many students also learn through the process of failing a previous placement what to say and 'how to play the game'. They may try to avoid showing their areas of weakness.

It is important that a practice teacher addresses the student's approach to the repeat placement early on and discuss this with him and his tutor. Appropriate financial advise and emotional support may have to be found. Similarly the boundaries for the new practice teaching relationship need to be set, for example, a student may need to express his feelings about the first placement. These should be accepted as inevitable and understandable, but they should not be allowed to block the progress of a second. At an early stage a student may have to decide whether he can put his feelings aside sufficiently to move on and engage with a new placement and to work with his second practice teacher.

It is often helpful if a student realises that this second placement is a new setting, a reassessment providing him with extra time and opportunity to practice skills, which is often all that is needed to develop the necessary competence.

Parochialism

Ever-increasing financial pressure on students is leading to a tendency for them to attend local Programmes. This particularly applies to students with family responsibilities and commitments, as they often require a course which does not involve much travelling. The situation may arise where students have little opportunity to take placements outside their own locality, or, if in employment, their own agency. Students who do want to travel from their course centre to a placement in another part of the country in order to broaden their experience, may find this impossible, due to the current pressure on placements with 'ringfencing' placement policies between university and local agency.

It is not unknown for students who are financially sponsored by an agency to attend their own local programme and to have both placements within their employing agency. This situation can impact on the placement and in particular pose difficulties for the practice teacher network, which is often a small and closeknit one. It means confidentiality has to be very closely guarded and a real effort made to ensure objectivity in assessment:

- Students can sometimes be known by reputation before a placement starts, or have in fact worked with the practice teacher in another capacity, as an unqualified worker in the field or residential sector
- Financially supported students are nominated for training by their line managers who subsequently have expectations on the practice teacher and placement setting to which their staff member turned-student goes. This situation may cause conflict, particularly if the student fails. Though not inevitable, the potential for conflict needs awareness and management by a practice teacher.

Activity 8.2   Problems on placement

Content: discussion exercise
Resources needed: facilitators
Time needed: 30 minutes

This activity provides an opportunity to consider the kind of situation which could occasionally occur on placement where the student is in his own employing agency. It should be done with a group of practice teachers working in pairs initially and then sharing ideas with the whole group.

Case Study

Sara is a new practice teacher undertaking training on the Award course. She has, with a lot of support from her mentor and the course group failed her student, who is an experienced unqualified social work assistant from a neighbouring team. The student still does relief work in her previous work setting during the course vacations and went back to this after the failed placement ended. Sara met the student's line manager at a case conference and found his attitude to her slightly unfriendly. At her next supervision with her own senior, she finds that he, atypically, puts practice teaching on the agenda. She is told that it is time that her progress on the practice teacher course is discussed, as her line manager appreciates that she has found the recent placement difficult. She encounters a sympathetic but concerned approach which gives her the clear impression that her manager regards her as finding it difficult adapting to the role of practice teacher. The remark is made that this is surprising as Sara has always been seen as someone with managerial potential, but not all good practitioners can make this adjustment.

Discussion/reflection pointers

- How realistic is this situation? Could it happen?
- What can Sara do?
- What should the mentor's role be in this situation?
- Should Sara share this situation with her placement colleagues?
- Any other issues?

A close practice teacher network can produce particular difficulties of confidentiality. Practice teachers need to discuss and share their work with students in order to gain support and develop. They need however to be aware that others in the group may have, or could be working with their students in future, or that the student's line manager could be present in the group, in another capacity. The ground rules in respect to confidentiality therefore need to be carefully set and managed.

Activity 8.3   Dealing with problems

Content: problem-solving activity
Resources needed: prepared scenarios
Time needed: one hour

This activity can be done individually or as a group. It is designed to assist with the identification and resolution of the problems which the need for confidentiality and practice teacher support can produce.

The practice teacher(s) should:

- Think of a situation where you are unhappy with the way you have supervised your student. You shared this with your mentor and jointly developed an action plan for their resolution. Your mentor is attending her support group at the university. Your line manager is a member of this group. She may discuss her supervision of you. What ground rules regarding confidentiality do you wish/expect her to observe?

- Think of a situation where you have discussed with your student an aspect of her practice with which you are unhappy. You take this to your practice teacher support group. What ground rules regarding confidentiality should be observed?

- Think of a student who has passed a placement with you and now has moved to another placement in the same agency as you. You hear via the 'grapevine' that he is not doing well. His practice teacher rings you and wants to discuss his progress with you. What do you do?

- Think of a situation where you have failed a student. The student is applying for relief work in the same agency during the university vacation. The line manager to whom application is made has heard that the student failed. She rings you informally for a reference without the student's knowledge. What do you do?

Student problems

Current funding policies for students and the reduction of some agencies' financial support for staff wishing to undertake the DipSW can cause considerable difficulties for students. The current trend for many social work courses to attract mature students means they may have family responsibilities and financial commitments. They may incur a real financial struggle to enter social work training. This can impact on placements as students:

- May need to work in their spare time
- May have difficulty affording appropriate clothes for placement
- May need placements to be flexible around child-care arrangements otherwise the costs become prohibitive
- May experience physical or mental illness and struggle to stay on the placement because they cannot afford to take time out. Students may have a history of mental illness but do not share it through fear, rightly or wrongly, of being the victims of oppressive attitudes, even during times when they are well and able to cope with the normal demands of life
- May need transport to and on placement but cannot afford to maintain reliable cars
- May face additional problems with work, child-care arrangements, if placement starts are delayed; extensions or repeat placements may be needed
- May experience personal crises with adolescents or elderly parents whilst on placement, relationship/family breakdown, ill-health, bereavement.

These kinds of situations can lead to a highly pressurised student struggling to complete the placement against tremendous odds. It is with this background that a practice teacher must operate, and often with a student pressing to complete placements within tight time-scales. The pressure to give the benefit of the doubt to a marginal student whose competence is not fully evidenced can be great. Similarly, an unwaged student has no potential for taking paid sick leave or compassionate leave. A practice teacher sometimes has to manage a situation where she knows a student desperately needs a break, and without it, is facing too many pressures external to the placement, to manage it. It will inevitably be up to the practice teacher to take a lead role in calling a meeting of tutor, student and agency representative to discuss time out for the student, or time-scales which will reduce the pressure. The practice teacher should also consider the potential for the placement becoming a part-time one to assist the student in completing it. This has implications for the university and agency in regard to assessment deadlines and placement resourcing.

There is often much that can be done to relieve the pressure on the student, but a practice teacher needs to be clear as to the various options available and be able to manage the situation as regards the service users and her own workload to ensure sufficient flexibility. It also means taking the firm line that standards are important and the student must prove competence, and that circumstances mitigating against this are managed to allow him the opportunity to do so.

Award training is jeopardised

Many practice teachers are undertaking their own training for the CCETSW Practice Teaching Award whilst supervising students. Occasionally, the need to fail a student can obstruct their progress with their award work in a way which can be frustrating and cause anxiety. Award work requires a practice teacher to undertake an assessed placement with a DipSW student. As part of this process, a practice teacher must be observed directly by her mentor and also in audio/videotape sessions. Student failure can impact on this in several ways:

- Placement is suspended or terminated before completion
- Student sabotages the direct observation or video work by not turning up
- Student is obstructive and difficult in observed sessions and does everything possible to try and ensure the practice teacher fails it
- Student refuses to comply with the direct observation, complaining that it puts extra pressure on them
- Student challenges the mentor's presence, regards her as conspiring with the practice teacher to fail him, tries to suck the mentor into assessing him and complains to the mentor about the practice teacher.

In many instances, if a student who is failing resists cooperation with the Award work it is impracticable to use the placement for this purpose. Often the additional time demands and stress of failing students obviate against it. A mentor's role can also change to being more of an informal second opinion to the practice teacher which can blur the process. Practice teachers therefore can become concerned that their student's failure may mean they too fail to become accredited.

The reality is that a student's failure can necessitate a delay and a post-ponement of the award work until another student placement can be offered. Although frustrating, this need not have lasting repercussions. A practice teacher can work out with her mentor and course centre a strategy for dealing with the situation. Extensions for the date of portfolio submission can be allowed and there is much scope for flexibility. Similarly work with failing students can be used for the portfolio, as its focus is not the student's competence but the practice teacher's skills and her capacity to reflect on them.

What if practice teacher and student do not get on?

The possibility of a personality clash between themselves and their student is one which frequently concerns practice teachers, and often unnecessarily. In any placement, practice teachers may find they are incompatible with their student in learning style and as people. This is not necessarily a situation which cannot be worked with constructively. The area of concern for practice teachers usually focuses on the subjectivity of their assessment role, and whether they are allowing their dislike of a student to affect their judgement. This concern can often lead practice teachers into being too lenient. Conversely, they can also worry that they like their student are being too easy or even too hard because of this.

Concerns can often be aggravated in Fail placements where any weakness can be tested and relationships deteriorate. It is almost inevitable that any student, even if intellectually accepting the validity of the failure will feel resentful, hurt and rejected. If unacknowledged and not addressed, this can lead to destructive relationships.

Lack of placement choice and pre-placement time reduces the chance to 'match' a student and practice teacher. The time available for them to get to know each other, and to discuss mutual expectations regarding supervision and approaches to learning is reduced with the result that any irreconcilable differences which would prevent their working together might not be identified.

Practice teachers can agonise unnecessarily over the issue of incompatibility. This is not to say that it is not positive that consideration is given as to whether personal biases and feelings are affecting assessment decisions, but anxiety about this needs to be contained. The practice teacher can check out her response with others when assessing. Also the focus of DipSW assessment is performance and how the student behaves in practice. Similarly a practice teacher has to substantiate her judgement. All these factors count as checks against irrational likes/dislikes affecting the situation.

Practice teachers, as social work practitioners, are often adept and experienced at professionally managing personal feelings for service users when making decisions. Initially in an unfamiliar educational situation, where the student is ever present in the work setting and in a colleague role, they do not recognise the similarity and the transferability of these skills. Once this is done, the need for support and the development of a strategy for managing incompatibility as one of the various difficulties placements can present, becomes easier.

In the management of all the various difficulties placements can present, it is important for a practice teacher to access the necessary support, and also to have some awareness of her own personal learning needs and readiness to work with students who fail.

Exercise 8.1   Dealing with problems in placement

Content: discussion exercise and role play
Resources needed: facilitators, model of a scenario, video camera
Time needed: one and a half hours

The aims of this exercise are to:

- Focus on problems which can occur on placements
- Develop an understanding of roles within an agency/university partnership
- Examine potential power conflicts between tutor and practice teacher.

This exercise is for use with a group of practice teachers. The course facilitators should model or use a video of a scenario where a tutor is unsupportive to the practice teacher and does not take the problems identified by her seriously. One sample scenario is outlined below. Similarly practice teachers could be asked to present similar problem situations from their own experience, in advance of the workshop. If modelled, volunteers from the group can participate. After watching the scenario, the group should discuss it and the issues raised.

Scenario

Interim evaluation meeting: the practice teacher has identified a student as having difficulties, and doubts that he will make the necessary progress before the placement ends. The areas of difficulty are time management, as recording is not up to date, and engaging with service users, as the student is over-anxious and lacks confidence to the point of totally avoiding conflict.

Practice teacher

The practice teacher has four years' social work experience and is taking her second student who is on a first placement. She works in a day centre for people with learning disabilities. Her colleagues are supportive and share her reservations about the student. She is doubtful about her teaching abilities, but can give clear reasons for the lack of competence and has made every effort to assist the student. She is a bit in awe of the tutor and tends to defer to his judgement as the expert. She wants the outcome of the meeting to be a formal recognition that failure could occur, with a remedial plan actioned and a further meeting to review it.

Student

The student is female, early thirties with experience as a care assistant. Her background is non-academic and she is very pressurised at home. She is a single parent, with financial difficulties, due to taking the course, and conflicting demands on her time. She thinks her lack of progress on the placement is her practice teacher's fault, because she should teach her how to be a social worker and that some of the cases where she has failed to deal with conflict are too difficult for her. She constantly refers to the positive remarks about her practice which she has received from supervisors in the past and other colleagues on the placement.

Tutor

Male and very academic in his approach, the tutor has not worked regularly with this placement. He and the practice teacher have only met once prior to this meeting. His approach is slightly patronising, as he is aware of the practice teacher's inexperience. He is very busy and harassed. He does not deny the problems in the student's practice but is a bit impatient with them, as the student's academic progress is satisfactory. A repeat placement will be very difficult to find. He clearly wants the practice teacher to carry on and resolve the student's difficulties and identify the problems for a second placement to resolve, when the student should hopefully get an experienced practice teacher. The outcome of this meeting is that the tutor prevails. No further meeting is agreed. He gives the impression that time prevails against this. Progress is recorded as satisfactory. The practice teacher is not happy and is left feeling that her practice teaching is inadequate.

Discussion pointers

- Is this scenario totally unrealistic?
- What does the practice teacher do now?
- What should she have done?
- Discuss the process in the modelling and how the practice teacher was disempowered
- Any other issues?

After discussion, this scenario could be re-enacted using volunteers from the group showing the practice teacher acting more assertively and implementing some of the ideas from the group.

Exercise 8.2   More work with placement problems

Content: discussion exercise
Resources needed: facilitators, prepared examples for discussion
Time needed: one hour

This exercise is for a group of practice teachers and identifies instances of difficulties on placement for them to discuss in pairs and then feedback, outlining the situation to the whole group and sharing ideas strategies for resolution. The situations for discussion should be on cards which can be passed around the groups. They can discuss one, several or all depending on time available:

- You are a practice teacher whose student has just started a second placement with you. Her first placement report was satisfactory. At a case conference a colleague who is from the student's first placement tells you that the student's work is very poor and her practice teacher should never have passed her. The student is not present and you are chatting informally after the meeting. What do you do?

- You are at a practice teacher workshop and share concerns about your student's practice. Her first placement practice teacher is present. Afterwards he tells you that he had concerns also. However he advises you against attempting to fail the student, as universities blame you and make it difficult. He tells you to go slow on the student as she has real family problems. What do you do?

- Your student has just completed his first placement with you, which he passed. You visit one of the cases he had and the service user makes it clear that he did not visit her, although he had recorded it. Her comment is that he will never make a social worker. What do you do?

Box 8.1   Procedures in the event of a malpractice allegation by a student on placement (from the Nottingham Trent University DipSW Practice Teacher Handbook, 1998)

1. The agency representative should bring the evidence of alleged malpractice to the attention of the tutor.
2. The tutor, module leader, agency representative and the student should meet as soon as possible to discuss the allegations of malpractice and the future course of action.
3. The student should be required to discontinue the placement until the allegations are investigated in the agency.
4. The agency representative should inform the tutor/module leader, in writing of the outcome of the investigation. Should the allegation be substantiated, the agency representative should advise what course of action would have to be taken if the student had been an employee of the agency.
5. In the event of the allegation not being substantiated the student should return to the placement. A meeting should take place between the tutor, the practice teacher and the student to consider the impact of the investigation upon the student's learning and any appropriate action, which may need to be taken to allow the placement to continue in the unusual way.
6. In the event of the allegation being substantiated, the student should not return to the placement.
7. The evidence of the alleged malpractice and the agency responses should be presented to the Practice Assessment Panel for consideration with the student's practice report.
8. The Practice Assessment panel may recommend to the external assessor that the original pass recommendation respect of the student should be reconsidered.
9. All the above documentation should be sent to at least one external examiner.
10. The agency representative/practice teacher is invited to attend the meeting with the external assessor on the day of the Assessment Board.
11. The student may submit written evidence to the Chair of the Assessment Board at least seven days before the date of the meeting.

---

9 Ready or not?

When is a practice teacher ready to work with a failing student?

Any placement can potentially have a Fail outcome, yet still reflect some highly effective practice teaching. Similarly, few students, even if successfully completing their placement, do not experience some sense of failure as part of the learning process. It therefore assists students if a practice teacher deals confidently with the likelihood of failure, mistakes and the recognition that no practice will be perfect.

A practice teacher needs therefore some idea of her readiness to work with failure. This requires an insight into her own training and development needs in this area. Awareness of her own motivation to practice teach, style, competence, and the level of expertise she considers necessary when failing a student, can help a practice teacher feel more confident and informed when faced with the likelihood of failure.

It can present itself in various ways, all of which require some prompt placement management, and a practice teacher who is ready to deal with it. For example, there may be no identified difficulties when the student comes to the placement. Students' potential for poor practice is often not identified in advance of the first placement, which often comes fairly early on the course. Students' selection for the course is the main yardstick for agencies accepting them on placement. New, inexperienced practice teachers often opt for first placements because they feel these can be less challenging. This is not necessarily so. Core skills in a first placement are crucial and must be passed. It is useful if practice teachers recognise the major responsibility first placements put upon them. They represent the first assessment of the

171

student's social work competence to practice, at a stage in the course when little is known about this. Indeed a case could be made, in respect to placement coordination, for the allocation of first placement students to experienced and Accredited Practice teachers, rather than at second placement stage which is the more usual practice. First placements often reflect a situation where if failure occurs, a repeat placement if offered is best undertaken at this stage.

The situation may arise where there may be no prior indication that a student's practice is weak. A student may arrive on a placement with a satisfactory or even 'glowing' reputation and first placement report. Occasionally, potential failure is not recognised on a first placement because assessment has not been thorough, or the difficulties avoided by mutual collusion between all participants. Similarly, a student with no previous identified difficulties may present them in a different placement setting and at a different stage of the course. A student's personal circumstances can change and create difficulties which prevent successful functioning on a placement.

Pressure on placement availability is great and it is always more difficult to find placements for students who have obviously struggled on a first one. This occasionally results in a situation where the university has not fully shared information with a practice teacher in advance of their meeting the student.

Usually a practice teacher is advised in advance that a student on a first placement has presented considerable difficulty. Similarly a practice teacher may be approached by a placements coordinator, and asked to offer a repeat placement for a student who has failed a previous one because her expertise is recognised. Such requests are flattering and by all means to be accommodated if the practice teacher feels able to undertake this essential work. However, preparatory work is needed before the decision can be made as to whether a practice teacher and placement are ready and resourced for this task. First, such requests should be accompanied by the previous practice teacher's report, outlining the student's development needs, so that a second practice teacher can decide whether her placement can meet them. In addition, a practice teacher should also expect some feedback from the university on the Assessment Board's decision, the reason why a repeat placement was agreed, with an outline of expectations as to what it will achieve. This helps a practice teacher decide whether she has the skills, experience, time and placement setting to undertake the placement. It is reasonable to ask the tutor why the second placement was agreed if this information is not available.

Training needs

A practice teacher needs to be prepared for any student to fail a placement. It is therefore important that practice teacher training addresses the issue of student failure, and a practice teacher is aware of her own training needs in this area. There can be a tendency for practice teacher training courses and programme workshops to avoid the issue of failure, reinforcing a general tendency to deny it on placements.

Alternatively, when addressed, failure can be treated as a peripheral part of the placement, or a discrete training area separate from the entire training or placement preparation process. The focus can also be on individual student's difficulties and not the overall problems which can be encountered in placement management.

Activity 9.1   Identifying training needs for work with failing students

Content: training needs exercise
Resources: copies of exercise
Time needed: one hour

This exercise is designed to enable practice teachers to identify their training needs and to include work with failing students within this identification, as well as a development action plan. It can be completed independently, by two practice teachers meeting together for mutual support, or by a practice teacher in discussion with a mentor or line manager.

- What training have you received already as a practice teacher?
- Did it address the area of work with failing students? If so was it:

Very good	Good	Adequate	Poor	Ignored

- Which would you find most difficult:
    Making the decision to fail
    Telling the student
    The process of telling the student
    Liaison with the tutor
    Liaison with colleagues
    Liaison with line managers
    Meeting the external examiners

- Do you consider your knowledge of the assessment procedures regarding failure:

Very good   Good   Adequate   Inadequate
- -

- Can you identify any specific training needs for work with failing students?

  Recording skills
  Report writing
  Evidence collection
  Giving feedback
  Challenging
  Confrontation
  Teaching anti-oppressive practice
  Disengaging
  Dealing with loss
  Managing placement reconstruction
  Identifying suitable learning opportunities
  Identifying student learning needs
  Assessment
  Appropriate work selection
  Teaching theory

- Select one aspect of the task of failing a student, for example, assessment. Break down the task into the following:

Knowledge   Skills   Attitudes

Ring in blue the areas in which you think you are strong and in red those in which you think you are weak

Action plan:

Outline three key areas you most need to develop to improve your skills with a failing student:

1.
2.
3.

Practice teachers also need to develop awareness of their own attitudes and responses to failure, and what feelings they may bring from their own personal and educational experiences which might aid or block successful practice teaching in this area. Anxieties and difficulties around failure can be more effectively managed, if they are recognised, acknowledged and discussed with a mentor or other appropriate person in the practice teacher's support system.

Activity 9.2 Engaging with failure

Content: self-development exercise
Resources needed: copy of exercise
Time needed: one hour

This activity should be done independently by a practice teacher and ideally shared with a mentor or colleague. It aims to assist a practice teacher with examining personal experiences/attitudes to failure, and with the identification of personal development needs for work with failing students.

1. Think of a situation where you have failed at something, in your own educational/social work training/personal life.

   - How did you respond?
   - How did your family respond?
   - How did your teacher/supervisor respond?
   - How did your peers respond?

2. How do you describe your attitude towards failure in yourself, for example, are you punitive, shameful, tolerant?
3. How do you describe your attitude towards failure in others, for example, partner, children, colleagues, staff?
4. In your workplace how is failure viewed by:

   - Your colleagues?
   - Your line manager?

5. How is failure viewed in your culture?
6. In what aspects of your life is success most important to you, for example, relationships, finance?
7. Think how your gender, age, race, faith, sexual orientation, class, disability might affect your approach to failure

8. How does your own experience of failure:

    ● Assist you in working with students?
    ● Cause blocks for you?

9. Do you think the aims of social work conflict with the task of failing a student:

Often   Sometimes   Never
- -

10. Identify your three main strengths and weaknesses in working with failure.
11. Identify three main development areas in working with failure. How can they be met?

Team Readiness

A practice teacher who is experienced and feels ready to accept a failing student on a placement needs also to consider her placement team and how ready it is. She may need to undertake some preparation work with her colleagues, before it is viable to accept a failing student. This decision needs to be discussed with her line manager, so he or she is involved in it, particularly if the team or service users might be affected adversely in the initial stages of the placement.

Similarly consideration needs to be given as to the team's ability to absorb any potential upset the student's subsequent failure might bring, if the resit placement is unsuccessful. The issue of failure needs inclusion in preparation for all placements, but specific work may be needed, when it is definitely identified that a student might fail, to ensure thorough assessment and positive learning opportunity can be provided. Areas for consideration may include:

● Experience of taking students – The practice teacher may be experienced, but needs to consider whether the team has also offered placements before, so there is some prior indication of how they manage. A first student, already known to have difficulties, may not be an appropriate student for the team to start with. Much will depend on what the student's weak areas are and their cause
● Staffing levels and workloads – Factors such as vacancy, leave or

sickness in the team need to be considered, as well as whether any existent team members are being supported through a crisis, such as bereavement or divorce

- Office accommodation – Does the student need to sit with the practice teacher and in the same room?
- Team integration of the practice teacher – Is she part of a large social work team, or in an isolated setting, or attached to a multidisciplinary team, with the potential for student mistakes or hostility to cause difficulties?
- Cohesion of team support and support offered managerially for placements – It is important that the team is committed to student training and does not just leave it to colleagues who enjoy practice teaching
- Team relationship with the practice teacher – It is useful to consider whether there are any unresolved conflicts which might lead to team members colluding with the student. Similarly, whether the team will be able to provide open and honest feedback, and accept that the practice teacher will evaluate this and make the assessment decision, even if it is one with which the colleague disagrees. Any unresolved conflicts within the team need careful consideration and resolution if possible. They do not necessarily prohibit a student who might fail from having the placement, but there is always a possibility that a failing student will try to exploit any weaknesses in the team. Any tension and conflicts need to be manageable in this situation
- Thought is needed as to the location of the student's previous placement and whether it and the practice teacher work together regularly. If so, whether this would present any insurmountable difficulties for accepting a student in this new placement.

Activity 9.3 Team readiness to take a failing student

Content: team exercise
Resources: copies of map, flipchart
Time needed: one hour

This activity can be done by a practice teacher with her team or jointly with the team manager as part of preparation for taking a student.

At a team meeting ask the team to list on a flipchart their assumptions about students. Put this list up in the room. Present the team with a list such as in the example given which makes assumptions about how failing students could present themselves:

- Anxious and vulnerable
- Demoralised
- Ashamed
- Badly taught
- Resentful
- Likely to make mistakes
- Unmotivated
- Finds learning difficult
- Unappreciative
- Personal and financial problems.

Ask the group to compare lists and if a discrepancy exists, could they work with it? Think about what characteristics in a team would be positive and contra-indicators for it being able to work with a student who is failing. On the map below some are listed. Add others as appropriate to your particular team. With a red pen, draw in the negative indicators which would apply to your team. With a blue pen, draw in the positive ones.

Keen to take students

Cohesion   Staff vacancies

    Inexperienced with students

                              Pressurised

        Team

Line manager disinterested

                    Fully staffed

Practice teacher isolation   Good admin

Overwork

    Dislike taking students   Experienced with students

Realistic workload

Supportive line manager   Overcrowded office

      Well-accommodated   Poor admin

Once your map is completed, consider what can be done to change the negative indicators. Take a large sheet of paper and write on it the red indicators which apply to your team. Rate them 0–5, with 5 indicating that nothing can be done to remove it. Focus on the indicators which have the lower scores and think of possible strategies to reduce or remove them.

If it is considered that a team is ready to provide the necessary support to a failing student and his practice teacher, preparation work is still necessary with the team, to build on this readiness. For example, a strategy is needed as to how much the team is told about the student. It will be necessary to share that the student failed a previous placement or had difficulties, in order to engage the team in the discussion as to whether a placement can be offered. This will inevitably raise queries as to the reason. A practice teacher needs therefore to think out in advance how much can be disclosed.

The previous practice teacher report and relevant Assessment Board feedback should be made available to the practice teacher and her line manager, whilst the decision about whether to take the student is being made. It should only be shared with other team members on a strictly need-to-know basis. For example, a team will need general reassurance on areas such as the student's safety to work with service users and whether any particular cases would be inappropriate or unsuitable.

Ideally, with this and all information, the student's knowledge and consent should be obtained. The student is of course free to share with team members once a placement starts, as he wishes, any views or feelings regarding his practice and progress on the course.

Practice teacher style and preferences

When dealing with all placements, matching of student and placement, which hopefully occurs at the placement coordination stage, is facilitated if a practice teacher is aware of her own competence and development needs, as well as the learning opportunities within her placement, and any student specification for the particular placement. It is particularly useful when this includes knowledge of her own and the placement's readiness to work with the area of failure. This can facilitate a student being placed with a practice teacher, who is best suited to respond confidently to the prospect of failure, rather than view it as an issue which is feared, avoided or addressed as a last resort.

Many practice teachers are experienced, highly competent and able to fail students successfully, but have differing responses to the prospect.

The matching process can be assisted if a practice teacher has reflected around her motivation to practice teach and the job satisfaction she gains from it, as well as her style, willingness and competence to work with failure.

Some practice teachers will feel strongly that experience of student training is necessary before work with a failing student can be undertaken, and that it is an impossible task to ask a first-time practice teacher to undertake. Others may feel more confident to do it in the early stages of their practice teaching career, providing they have the benefits of the Award training, and support systems are in place. A practice teacher who feels inexperienced and not ready to work with a failing student should be prepared to refuse. An anxious, uncertain, practice teacher is not going to help a student who is probably at a similar stage.

However there may still be a variety of responses amongst experienced practice teachers to taking a student, identified as failing, dependent on their motivation and style in respect to practice teaching:

- A practice teacher may feel competent and be experienced in failing students but prefer not to undertake the task, because training is a peripheral activity to her job and she only takes one student at time. She offers student placements because she enjoys the stimulation, exchange of ideas, facilitation of learning with students who make rapid and considerable progress
- Another practice teacher may welcome a range of students as regards competence and pace at which they learn
- A practice teacher may prefer sometimes to work with a student who needs extra attention, and is satisfied with slower progress and the development of her skills in giving negative feedback. This task has challenges and satisfactions of its own and some awareness by a practice teacher in the area of motivation and style can assist in placement management. (Exercise 9.1 at the end of this chapter provides an opportunity to reflect on this.)

The social work profession has a responsibility to train its recruits successfully and eliminate those who are unsuitable. Placement pressures and coordination processes may inevitably prevent a practice teacher from always working with the kinds of students they prefer and who meet their own development needs. However, an awareness of these, which includes the issues around failure, increases the likelihood of good matching and effective well-managed placements for failing students.

The provision of high-quality placements requires attention to this aspect of social work training. A successful placement does not always pass its student. Failure on a social work course is not a disgrace, nor is a practice teacher who fails a student incompetent herself – often quite the reverse. The whole topic does however need recognition and integration within practice teacher training and placement coordination systems, so that failing students can be placed with practice teacher best able to provide the necessary training.

Practice teachers working with failing students are unlikely to enjoy the process but can experience it as a challenging one which stretches their skills to the full. Certainly a successful placement can have a Fail outcome, just as the exhilaration of success and the pain of failure can be inextricably linked. As part of the learning process they exist in all placements.

Exercise 9.1 Ready or not?

Content: self-development exercise
Resources needed: exercise
Time needed: 45 minutes

This is a self-development exercise which focuses the attention of a practice teacher on why they undertake the job and whether their motivation/needs can be met in work with failing students.

General expectations/motivation

1. I undertake practice teaching because ....
2. What I find most satisfying about practice teaching is ....
3. What I find least satisfying about practice teaching is ....

Specific expectations in respect to failing students

1. Can the satisfaction you gain from practice teaching be met by a failing student?
   If yes, how?
   If not, why not?

2. I would think that a student's failure represents my failure as a practice teacher

   Yes   Sometimes   Never
- -

3. I would expect that the DipSW selection process should be able to take on students who can pass

    Always   Seldom   Never

- -

4. Do you think that as a profession we are stringent on our entrance requirement?

    Very stringent   Stringent   About right   Lenient   Very lenient

- -

5. I would be able to deal with the situation where a student:

- Refused to accept my fail decision

    1   2   3   4   5

- -

    Very badly   Very
                                                                 confidently

- Made accusations regarding my competence

    1   2   3   4   5

- -

    Very badly   Very
                                                                 confidently

- Made a formal complaint about me, which I consider unjustified

    1   2   3   4   5

- -

    Very badly   Very
                                                                 confidently

- Criticised my competence informally to his tutor

    1   2   3   4   5

- -

    Very badly   Very
                                                                 confidently

- Criticised my competence informally to my colleagues

    1   2   3   4   5

- -

    Very badly   Very
                                                                 confidently

6. How ready do you think you are to work with a student who is failing?

| 1 | 2 | 3 | 4 | 5 |

Very ready   Not ready

7. If you do not feel ready to work with a failing student outline your three main development areas
    1.
    2.
    3.

8. If you think you are competent to work with a failing student would you want to do it?
    If not, why not?

9. Consider the profile below and complete one for the student(s) you have supervised within the past five years:

Name	*Age*
Gender	*Race*
Sexual orientation	*Dis/ability*
Academic background	*Dipsw Programme*
Learning style	*MA/BA/DipHE*
Social work background	*Competence*
Pre-course experience	*Personality*
Learning blocks presented	*Placement outcome – Pass/Fail*

10. Consider the profiles and whether you think they represent a broad range of student experience. Are there any major gaps?

Bibliography

Ahmad, B. (1990) *Black Perspective in Social Work*, Birmingham: Venture Press.

Anderson, M., Osada, N. and Thompson, B. (1990) *Practice Teaching in Social Work*, Birmingham: Pepar.

Argyle, M. (1981) *Social Skills and Health*, London: Methuen.

Ashmed, S., Hallett, C., Stratham, D. and Watts, S. (1988) 'A Code of Practice', *Social Work Education*, 7: 2.

Ashworth, P. and Saxton, J. (1990) 'On Competence', *Journal of Further and Higher Education*, 14: 2.

Baird, B. (1994) 'The Proof of the Pudding: A Study of Clients' Views of Students Competence', *Social Work Education*, 10: 1–2.

Barnett, R. (1994) *The Limits of Competence*, Buckingham: The Society for Research into Higher Education and the Open University.

BASW (1995) *'Whistleblowers': Guidance for Social Services on Free Expression of Staff Concerns*, available from BASW, 16 Kent St, Birmingham.

Batti-Sinclair, K. (1992) 'Mentoring and Consultancy for Black Social Work Students', *Issues in Social Work Education*, 15: 2.

Borrill, W. (1991) *The Management and Reduction of Failing Placements*, Report to the Department of Health, Centre for Evaluative Studies and Developmental Research, University of Southampton.

Brandon, J. and Davies, M. (1979) 'The Limits of Competence in Social Work: The Assessment of Marginal Students in Social Work', *British Journal of Social Work*, 9: 3.

Broome, J. (1980) *The Objectives of a Law Degree Course: Are They Being Assessed?*, Aldershot: Gower Press.

Brummer, N. (1988) 'Cross Cultural Assessment: Issues Facing White Practice Teachers and Black Students', *Social Work Education*, 7: 2.

Bung, F.D., Lloyd, K.S. and Templeton, B. (1982) 'Competence in Medicine', *Medical Teacher*, 4.

Butler, B. (1979) 'Who Needs Field Work Training?', *Community Care*, pp. 22–4.

Callendar, C., Toyne, J., Connor, H. and Spilsbury, M. (1993) *National and Scottish Vocational Qualifications: Early Indications of Employers Take-up and Use*, Report No. 259 of the Institute of Manpower Studies, Centre for Labour Market Studies: University of Leicester, pp. 69–83.

CCETSW (1989) *Improving Standards in Practice Learning*, Paper 26.3, London: Central.

CCETSW (1991, revised 1995) *Requirements and Regulations for the Diploma in Social Work*, Paper 30, London: Central.

CCETSW (1996) *Assessing Quality for Practice Teaching: Rules and Regulations for the Practice Teacher Award Course*, London: Central.

Cox, M. (1995) 'Whistleblowing in Social Work', *Professional Social Work*, April.

Curnock, K. and Prais, H. (1982) 'An Approach to Fieldwork Assessement', *British Journal of Social Work*, 12.

Danbury, H. (1994) *Teaching Practical Social Work*, Aldershot: Arena.

Danbury, H. (1983) *The Video Cassette Recorder – A Valuable Tool in Student Learning*, (unpublished).

Davies, M. (1979) 'Field Work Failure; A Rare Breed', *Community Care*, September, pp. 18–19.

Doel, M. Shardlow, S. Sawdon, C. and Sawdon, D. (1996) *Teaching Social Work Practice*, Aldershot: Arena.

Easton, S. and Van Larr, D. (1995) 'Experiences of Lecturers Helping Distressed Students in Higher Education', *British Journal of Guidance and Counselling*, 23: 2.

Evans, D. (1987) 'Live Supervision in the Same Room: A Practice Teaching Method', *Social Work Education*, 3: 13.

Evans, D. (1990) *Assessing Students' Competence to Practice in College and Practice Setting*, CCETSW London: Central.

Hager, P., Gonzi, A. and Athanasou, J. (1994) 'General Issues about Assessment of Competence', *Assessment and Evaluation in Higher Education*, 19: 1.

Hayward, C. (1979) *A Fair Assessment: Issues in Evaluating Course Work*, London: CCETSW.

Hodgkinson, P. (1992) 'Alternative Models of Competence in Vocational Education and Training', *Journal of Further and Higher Education*, 16: 2.

Humphrey, M. and Morton, J. (1991) 'A Model for Learning', *Social Work Education*, 1: 10.

Jessup, G. (1991) *Outcomes*, London: Falmer Press.

Kadushin, A. (1976) *Supervision in Social Work*, New York: Columbia University Press.

Knowles, M. (1984) *Andragogy in Action*, San Francicso: Jossey Bass.

Kubler-Ross, E. (1969) *On Death and Dying*, New York: MacMillan.

Marshall, K. (1991) 'NVQs: An Assessment of the Outcomes Approach to Education and Training', *Journal of Further and Higher Education*, 15: 3.

Milner, O. and O'Bryne, P. (1986) 'Impact of Failing Students on Tutors', *Social Work Education*, 1: 1.

Mitchell, L. (1993) *Assessment of Competency at Level 5*, Competence and Briefing Series, No. 8 (March) (CLMS, University of Leicester, Module 3, Unit 4).

Morrell, E. (1979) 'A Lesson in Assessment', *Community Care*, November, pp. 26–8.

NCVQ (National Council for Vocational Qualifications) (1988) *Agency Training Notes 1*, London: NCVQ.

O'Hagan, K. (ed.) (1996) *Competence in Social Work Practice*, London: Jessica Kingsley.

Owens, C. (1995) 'How Assessment of Competence in DipSW is Changing the Culture of Placements', *Social Work Education*, 12: 3.

Parsloe, P. and Stephenson, O. (1979) 'Social Work Training: The Struggle for Excellence', *Community Care*, 289, p. 30.

Pell, L. and Scott, D. (1995) 'The Cloak of Competence: Assessment Dilemmas', *Social Work Education*, 14: 4.

Phillips, M. (1996) *All Must Have Prizes*, London: Little Brown.

Powells, R. and S. (1994) 'Practice Makes Perfect', *Professional Social Work*, Mitchell Library.

Prais, S.J. (1991) 'Vocational Qualifications in Britain and Europe: Theory and Practice', *National Institute of Economic Review*, 136: May 1991 (CLMS, University of Leicester, Module 3, Unity).

Redfield Jamieson, K. (1996) *An Unquiet Mind*, London: Picador.

Roberts, T. (ed.) (1996) *To Fail Or Not To Fail*, Bradford and Ilkley Community College: West Riding Diploma in Social Work.

Symans, B. (1980) 'A Helping Hand for Assessment', *Community Care*, March, pp. 27–8.

Toussant, P., Yeardley, A. and Leyden, J. (1989) *Live Supervision*, London Borough of Hackney: SWE Unit.

Walker, J., McCarthy, P. and Timms, N. (1995) *In Pursuit of Quality: Improving Practice Teaching in Social Work*, University of Newcastle-on-Tyne.

Index

absence 121, 122, 125
Academic Review group 16
access to information 23–8
accountability 43
accreditation 9
Accreditation of Practice Teachers and Agencies 122
Accredited Practice teachers 172
activities
  breaking bad news 106–7
  ground rules 57–60
  minimum levels 85–6
  placement problems 144–6, 162–3
  preparation for direct observation 64–6
  self-awareness 87–8
  self-development 39–47
  student stereotypes 103–4
  support systems 135–7
  team readiness 177–9
  training needs 173–6
  tutors 126
  written reports 112–14
Agency Accreditation 126
andragogy 31
Anglian University Assets Programme 31
anxiety 119–20, 130
appeals 16–17, 23, 120, 148, 150
Approval of Agencies 12–14
Ashworth, P. 31
assessment 5–10, 119, 128

failure 29–49
function 33–4
practice teaching 11–28
task 36–8
Assessment Board 2, 9, 12, 14–15
  complaints procedure 17
  placement problems 143
  procedures 24, 33
  readiness 172
  record-keeping 111
  repeat placement 159
  support systems 128
  team readiness 179
Assuring Quality for Practice Teaching 123
attendance 9, 51
attitude 60–1, 100
audio recordings 55

bad news 106–8
Barnett, R. 31
Beckford, J. 5
black students 133–4
borderline cases 7, 80, 88–92
  anxieties 119–20
  bad news 108–10
  problems 164–5
  refusal to accept 146–50
  reporting failure 104–8
Borrill, WE. 150
breakdown of arrangements 156–7
breaking bad news 106–8
buddies 131–2

Callendar, C. 30
Care Sector Consortium 6
cause for complaint 18–20
CCETSW *see* Central Council for
    Education and Training in Social
    Work
Central Council for Education and
    Training in Social Work (CCETSW)
    5, 6, 12, 15
  assessment function 33, 35
  complaints procedure 17
  core skills 92
  direct observation 56
  good enough practice 81, 82
  guidelines 36, 84
  mentors 129
  practice skills 41
  Practice Teacher's Award 165
  practice teaching 7, 8–9
  revised requirements 16
  service users 69
  support systems 120, 123
Certificate in Social Services (CSS) 41
Certificate of Qualification in Social
    Work (CQSW) 5, 7–8, 41, 52, 110,
    125
change of placement setting 127
changes 6–10
child abuse 5
child-care 164
clothing 164
collection of evidence 51–3
communication 96
competence 6, 9, 47
  assessment 30–3, 51
  definition 34–8
complaints 17–18, 23, 122, 132
confidentiality 49, 66, 130, 134
  malpractice 155
  support systems 137
constraints in assessment 29–30
consultants 133–5
contracts 48–9, 99–100
core competences 55, 82, 92, 94
course leaders 24, 26
CQSW *see* Certificate of Qualification in
    Social Work
Credit Accumulation and Transfer
    Scheme (CATs) 124
CSS *see* Certificate in Social Services

culture 40
curriculum 54, 61, 81

Danbury, H. 53, 127, 151
Davies, M. 7
decision-making 33–4, 51–77
  mentors 129
  refusal to accept 146–50
  repeat placement 159
denigration 54
dilemmas 29–30, 80–1
Diploma in Social Work (DipSW)
  assessment 8–10, 11–28, 29, 33–4
  consultants 133
  history 6–8
  malpractice 155
  mentors 128
  Partnerships 31
  Placements Co-ordinator 126
  Practice Teacher's Award 165
  programme practice 21–2
  student problems 164–5
  support systems 120–1
  workshops 130
  written records 111–12
direct evidence 54, 55–66
direct observation 9, 14, 55–7
  feedback 63
  placement problems 165
  preparation 72, 74–7
  pro forma 68
disadvantaged students 133
disciplinary procedures 22–3
discrimination 134
Doel, M. 36, 56
double marking 123
dyslexia 38

effectiveness 38–43
emotional support 119
employers 5, 6
Employment for the 1990s 6
engagement 96
environment for assessment 38–43
Evans, D. 54-5
evidence 35, 51–3, 70
exercises
  cause for complaint 18–20
  contracts on assessment 48–9
  direct observation 72, 73, 74–6, 76–7

failing placement procedures 24–8
feedback 115–16
good enough practice 93–5, 95–6
placement problems 167–70
readiness 181–3
report writing 117–18
support systems 138
extension of placement 157–8
External Examiners 15–16, 24
external support systems 137–41

fail decision 33–4
failing placement procedures 23–8
feedback 9, 14, 51
bad news 109–10
direct observation 61, 63, 66–7
evidence 55
failing placement 143
indirect observation 70
line managers 121
mentors 129
potential failure 115–16
flagging 12, 60, 115, 150

good enough practice 71, 79–96
grapevine 101–2
grief 98, 119, 148, 150
ground rules 43–9, 57–60, 137
guidelines 12

Hager, P. 31
handbooks 35, 123
Hayward, C. 54
Heads of Department 15
hearing impediments 38
Hodgkinson, P. 31

illness 164
implementation procedures 119
independent counsellors 131
indicators 81, 83, 96
indirect observation 69–71
information access 23–8
interpersonal skills 70

Jessup, G. 31
judgement 120, 147

Kadushin, A. 81
knowledge 35, 41–2

Knowles, M. 31
Kubler-Ross, E. 105

language 39
Learning Agreement meetings 11, 16, 20
placement problems 156
record-keeping 99–100
support needs 124, 134
learning opportunities 127
Line Managers 23, 67–9, 70, 120–2
Local Authority Services Act 7
low failure rate 5, 8, 47

malpractice 23, 102, 122, 155–6, 157, 170
management of failing placement 143–4
market principles 6
Marshall, K. 31
mature students 97
mentors 64, 128–9, 165
mid-placement 56
Milner, O. 146, 148, 150
minimum levels 79–80
Mitchell, L. 31
mitigating circumstances 17–20
monitoring 56–7, 121, 124
Morrell, E. 7

National Council for Vocational
Qualifications (NCVQ) 6, 31, 34
National Vocational Qualification
(NVQ) 30–1, 33
NCVQ *see* National Council for Vocational Qualifications
needs in training 173
newly qualified workers 84
non-assessment 111

O'Bryne, P. 146, 148, 150
Observers 24
O'Hagan, K. 31–2, 34

Parkes, M. 148
parochialism 161
performance 89–90
personal crises 164
personal preparation 102–3
personality clashes 127–8, 166–7
Phillips, M. 36
placement 7, 9, 11, 35, 48, 84
adequacy 93

availability 172
evaluation section 12
failing procedures 23–8
problems 143–70
record-keeping 97, 98–104
reputations 102
shortages 153–4
support systems 120–1, 122–4
termination 23, 57, 157–8
Placements Co-ordinator 126–8
police checks 20–2
Powells, R. 30
Powells, S. 30
power issues 49
Practice Assessment Panel (PAP) 12–15,
    122
  repeat placement 159
  sample assessment report 27–8
  support systems 124
practice requirements 35
Practice Teacher Award 69
practice teachers 5, 7, 9
  assessment 8–10, 11–28
  direct observation 60–1
  evidence collection 51–2
  failing placement procedures 24, 25
  ground rules 43–9, 58
  minimum levels 91–2
  police checks 22
  profiles 100–1
  reactions 106
  readiness 171–2
  record-keeping 97–8
  second opinion 16
  sessions 37
  style 179–81
  support needs 119–42
  workshops 130–1
Practice Teacher's Award 128–9, 131,
    165–6
pre-placement 99, 123
preferences 179–81
preparation
  observation 57, 61–4, 64–6
  personal 102–3
problems 143–70
procrastination 105

racism 133
readiness 171–83

recommendations 17
record-keeping 97–118
reflective evidence 54, 62
Rehabilitation of Offenders Act 21
relationships 56–7, 127–8, 147, 164, 166–
    7
repeat placement 159–61
Requirements and Regulations 35
resistance 148
reviews 5–10
Roberts, T. 15, 16, 17, 98
rumours 101–2

satisfactory practice 79–80
Saxton, J. 31
second opinions 16, 130, 132, 159
second placement 84
Seebohm report 6
selection of work 53–5
self-awareness 86–8
service users 69, 94, 115, 121, 148, 155
  placement suspension 158
Social Service Departments (SSDs) 7,
    98
staff appraisal 122
standards 5, 80, 81, 88
style 179–81
success ethic 98
supervision 56, 98, 125
  models 43
  purposes 48
support 71, 90–1, 119–42
suspension of placement 157–8

teaching arrangement breakdown 156–
    7
team readiness 176–9
termination of placement 23, 57, 157–8
Thatcherism 6
traditional training methods 5
training 5–10, 173
transport 164
trouble-shooting 128
tutors 49, 70, 97, 122–6, 149–50
  contact 150–3
  failing placement procedures 24
  placement termination 157
  repeat placement 160

universities 123–4, 150–2

values 35
video recordings 55, 56, 69–71, 82, 129
    problems 165
    workshops 130
visual impairments 38

vocational training 6, 8

work selection 53–5
workshops 82, 130–1
written reports 9, 11–17, 110–12